"*The conflicts and irritations in our life is the Universe telling us that we are out of alignment with what is fully possible. In this highly practical and engaging book Ms. Labelle gives us insights into how we can insightfully turn our conflicts into positive productive energy.*"

Ian Percy, author of **Going Deep** and **The Profitable Power of Purpose**

Deciphering people... Finding out what is said and what is not... Confronting the undiscussable...This is what Ghislaine is best at. Plunge into her book and change forever the way you envision conflicts.

Alain Samson, author of **Make your own LUCK**

I0455972

"*First with a witness' eye and then with an expert's eye, Ghislaine Labelle knows exactly how to identify complex issues in conflict management and resolve them in an efficient way. Here at last is a book that takes us beyond the rhetoric and sets out a bold plan of action for actually addressing the roots of conflict management. Any HR professional or any manager that has to intervene with people needs read this book first.*"

Normand Richard

Transcontinental Northern California - Newspaper Group Director

Organizational Development and Human Resources

"In the last four years, I have had the privilege to collaborate with Ghislaine. She not only demystifies, for managers and team members, conflicting issues but she gives plenty of advices on how to prevent them. Written with a creative approach, CALMING THE WATERS AT WORK will certainly help you resolve difficulties whether you experience them at work, in your family or even on vacation!"

Marie-Claude Gagnon, M.A, M.A.P

Psychologist and Senior Counsellor

Continuing Education, University of Laval in Québec

University of Laval in Québec

CALMING
THE
WATERS
AT
WORK

How to Deal with Workplace Conflicts

CALMING
THE
WATERS
AT
WORK

How to Deal
with Workplace
Conflicts

Ghislaine Labelle
A True Story

Published by Advantage, Charleston, South Carolina.
Member of Advantage Media Group.

ADVANTAGE is a registered trademark and the Advantage colophon is a trademark of Advantage Media Group, Inc.

Printed in the United States of America.

ISBN: 978-1-59932-160-8
LCCN: 2009911077

This publication is designed to provide accurate and authoritative information in regard to the subject matter covered. It is sold with the understanding that the publisher is not engaged in rendering legal, accounting, or other professional services. If legal advice or other expert assistance is required, the services of a competent professional person should be sought.

Most Advantage Media Group titles are available at special quantity discounts for bulk purchases for sales promotions, premiums, fundraising, and educational use. Special versions or book excerpts can also be created to fit specific needs.

For more information, please write: Special Markets, Advantage Media Group, P.O. Box 272, Charleston, SC 29402 or call 1.866.775.1696.

Visit us online at **advantagefamily**.com

Acknowledgements

I want to express my appreciation to my friends and those who helped me succeed in completing this project and who lent themselves to reading my manuscript. From their invaluable commentaries, Yvan Grimard, Celine Labelle, Caroline Lampron and Sylvie Racine contributed to improving this book.

A big thank-you to Jean Pare, my editor (French version), who, once again, believed in my project and helped me find its direction.

I equally thank all of my clients, all those who participated in the bonding activities I head, the confidence they instilled in me toward this book, and their open-mindedness in solving their conflicts. Without their questions, it would have been difficult to present the vast subject that is conflict management in such a concise way.

PREFACE

Conflict Can Be Positive

Ever since writing *A Winning Team* in 2001, I have been helping those in charge with conflict resolution and crisis management. Without a doubt, many professionals work in an unhappy setting. Even more often, they suffer in silence for years before sending out the first S.O.S. Because of these issues, I had the idea of preparing a book aimed at managers who wish to defuse those budding conflicts and equip themselves to better navigate through the turbulent zones.

Allow me a small warning. *How to Resolve Conflict in the Workplace* does not present a tried-and-true method of conflict resolution. In order to resolve conflict, you must first rigorously diagnose the situation (as the old saying goes, "a problem defined is a problem half-solved"). It can be costly to apply a blanket remedy without taking into account the factors specific to your situation and the people involved. In fact, once you find yourself in the whirlpool that is conflict, you cannot proceed by just trying to erase mistakes. You must know how to address properly the unmet needs. And quickly.

Why do managers wait to intervene or act only once a conflict has exploded? Because they lack the time and expertise necessary to properly analyze their teams' behavior. However, we expect them to come up with solutions that will resolve any emerging conflict. After repeatedly witnessing the phenomenon of managers waiting to address conflict only after a certain time elapsed, I searched to find an explanation. What I found is rather simple. Very few people, managers included, understand what transpires between the first signs of friction within a group and the outbreak of a conflict. But, between those two situations are several milestones, interactions and reactions that reflect the decline of the interpersonal climate. Through this book, I hope to help managers quickly detect the precursors to conflict, as well as the deterioration of the relationships between their team members and the tense atmosphere that can arise, so that they can intervene before the situation worsens.

The source of conflict is rarely clear-cut. Because it relies on perspectives that are subjective and usually emotional, it is usually difficult to manage. It happens often, for example, that two individuals involved in a dispute will propose very different reasons for the origin of the problem and equally varied interpretations of the facts involved. Interestingly, those types of comments often lead to solutions, if we pay attention. Observe carefully what transpires in your workplace. Is there conflict between only two people or an entire team? This is an important guideline for your analysis of the conflict that may have already started.

Even if the goals of this book included offering clarity on the topic of conflict, know that even myself, as an expert on the matter, can face situations that are both uncharted and unexpected. Here is an example: I had the opportunity to spend a two-week holiday in Greece aboard a sailboat, the *Lilly*, amid passengers and staff whom I had never met. A serious conflict emerged between two members of the group, a group that I had started to consider a crew and team. This voyage taught me two things about conflict. But, as my work is precisely to help manage and prevent conflict year-round, I was determined to enjoy my vacation and *not intervene*. I wanted to *stay out of it!* In retrospect, I realized I was at fault. You will understand why once you read my book.

I equally learned something that was instrumental to my professional activities: Conflict can be broken down, or "dissected," into five discernible stages that will be described in the following chapter. As an introduction to each of these stages, I will share certain elements of my experience aboard the sailboat.

This brief tale of sailing, devoted to the persistent difficulties experienced by the *Lilly's* crew, clearly illustrates how conflict can degenerate. The stages mark the progressive deterioration of the climate and quality of the interpersonal relationships that we can observe during conflict. As one stage follows the other, the unmet needs multiply exponentially.

We must face the facts: The more we wait to act on an emerging conflict, the more the work environment will be contaminated by an unpleasant atmosphere. The more this deteriorates, the more complicated the situation becomes, making it more difficult to know how or where to intervene.

By sharing my passion and professional knowledge, I hope to help managers tame and dissect conflict, whose resolution is by far the most formidable challenge that can be given to human resources managers.

It may be hard to believe, but my ultimate goal is to teach you to *appreciate* conflict, as challenging as that may sound. If you open your eyes, you will notice more signs; if you intervene quickly, you will minimize the fallout; if you adopt a positive attitude about conflict, it becomes easier to manage and benefit from. Yes – I did say benefit! So, repeat after me: Conflict can be positive! If you remain skeptical, then you have just discovered the first of your convictions that you must shake off in order to learn to appreciate conflict.

Ghislaine Labelle, M.Ps., CHRP

FOREWORD

By Kenneth W. Thomas

Those of us who write about managing conflicts like to emphasize that they can be beneficial when handled constructively. But too often we see the destructive side of conflict. In particular, I have seen a number of work teams that were damaged by conflicts that escalated to the point where they tore the social fabric of the team and left it barely able to function. These unfolding escalations took on the apparent inevitability of a Greek tragedy at times, leaving team leaders with a sense of helplessness. Part of the difficulty was that the behaviors involved seemed irrational, so that the leader and other team members couldn't understand what was driving those behaviors—let alone, how to intervene constructively.

This is the first book I have seen that specifically explains the sequence of events in this deterioration—and what the team leader needs to do at each stage to reverse the process. Ghislaine Labelle gets beneath the apparent irrationality to pinpoint the series of unmet needs that keep team conflicts escalating—from individuals who feel excluded in some way, through the formation of factions with shared grievances, to survival-based estrangements and departures from the team. At each of five stages in this process, she points out the behavioral signs that can help leaders and team members recognize what's happening and, importantly, the remedial actions that can be taken.

I found this book to be remarkably insightful and useful, as well as highly readable. Ghislaine builds the book around an especially dramatic experience of team disintegration—during a lengthy sailing cruise. She shares that experience and many other examples from her previous consulting engagements to emphasize the need to take action to prevent unnecessary and destructive conflicts. All these examples give her book the strong ring of truth and will help readers apply the concepts to their own team situations to deal more efficiently with conflicts. This book fills an important gap in current leadership training, and I recommend it for team leaders at all levels.

Kenneth W. Thomas

www.kennethwthomas.net

Kenneth W. Thomas, Ph.D., has made distinguished contributions to the research literature on conflict management in organizations and developed widely-used training and intervention aides. He is co-author of the Thomas-Kilmann Conflict Mode Instrument and Introduction to Conflict and Teams and author of Introduction to Conflict Management, all published by CPP, Inc.

TABLE OF CONTENTS

INTRODUCTION

Analyzing conflict

In order to analyze conflict, you must first understand it. To be more specific, you must know how to detect its first signs and understand its dynamic and evolution. From its latent period until the final explosion, conflict develops in an underhanded manner. We can feel it looming, but we can't predict exactly when it will burst. The crisis results from an accumulation of numerous events or disagreeable situations, often unmanaged, that lead to a surplus of frustration and unvoiced feelings of the parties involved. This buildup produces devastating effects and drives the conflict's escalation and final explosion.

You can compare the subtle progression of an unmanaged conflict with that of an undiagnosed tumor. The more we wait, the higher the risk that the tumor will endanger other parts of our body. Personal conflicts behave this way too. To better keep cancer from spreading, you must adopt preventative measures (a healthy diet, stress management, regular medical exams) and be on the lookout for early symptoms. The same applies to conflict situations. By being aware of the indicators and symptoms, we can analyze potentially conflicting situations more efficiently and accurately.

Time is conflict resolution's worst enemy

An oft-believed statement is that "time heals all wounds," or that simply letting time elapse can fix any situation. This is entirely false in conflicting situations. In the scope of my interventions and the teams I have spoken to, I often repeat: "Time is the worst enemy of harmony." Too often, managers imagine that time will remedy difficult situations. On the contrary, time plays against the well-being and health of the personnel and company involved. The more that time elapses, the more the situation degenerates. So here is a general description of the five stages of conflict so that it can be recognized in timely fashion; I will describe them in more detail in the following chapters.

A brief description of the stages

1. *Exclusion:* This is a lack of commitment to include an individual, leader or sub-group within a team. This first stage does not necessarily drive conflict, but it does set the scene for the situation to head in that direction.

2. *Confrontation:* A clumsy expression of a person's needs and differences or a lack of recognition of different needs. Dissatisfied needs lead to frustration. Ignoring this normal step in the development of a team can lead to a sterile confrontation of needs, interests and values. By not acting on this stage, a manager favors the emergence of conflict.

3. *The Formation of Factions:* Collusion between members of a team in which the bond is formed because of mutual dissatisfaction, grievances or empathy. Clans exist because of confrontation with the opposing party. At this stage, the

team is more and more inundated with conflict, which is now increasingly critical and affecting more people.

4. *Escalation and Explosion:* Open confrontation accompanied by hurtful and possibly abusive intentions, reflecting the adoption of a win-or-lose approach. Because there is a break in communication between the members of two clans, the manager will often play the role of messenger between the two. In most cases, wrongdoing will be present. The objective of those involved in conflict is to win at all costs. Participants can use certain strategies particularly to make the opposing team lose its lead or wound it. As the saying goes, "All's fair in love and war." The resulting climate becomes unbearable.

5. *Estrangement:* The collapse of the team, either literally or figuratively. This can be due to team members' departing or a total lack of rapport between colleagues, which can lead to complete avoidance. I can tell you that it is not easy to be the manager in this picture; it may be impossible to rekindle the team spirit and confidence. Just like the disaster zone of a natural catastrophe, the damage is extensive.

Test your intuition

After this quick summary of the five stages of conflict, try to test your intuition by trying the following exercise (just for fun!). Note that the symptoms listed are reported to the manager within the context of a team, but can equally apply to a relationship between two people.

Assign each of the following symptoms to the stage you believe it applies to the most. The answers can be found at the bottom.

Stages:

1. Exclusion

2. Confrontation

3. Formation of Factions

4. Escalation and Explosion

5. Estrangement

Symptoms:

A. Before an important meeting, I need to meet with the subgroups that have formed in order to prevent quarrels that may get out of hand.

B. Before the arrival of new players, I sense unease between certain people; this is a situation that may be difficult to manage.

C. The members of my team are constantly walking into my office to unload about their conflicts and the frustrations that cause tension between them and their colleagues. I can no longer hold team meetings. The climate is tainted with distrust, and hostility is openly expressed.

D. I have serious problems managing my time. There are individuals who avoid each other and refuse to work together. It's such a hassle to try and find solutions based on ensuring that certain people don't work together.

E. At work, some members of my team clash on their ideas, needs, and values. I am afraid that these debates will have serious consequences, as they do not seem to converge towards a solution.

Are these symptoms present in your workplace?

In order to figure out whether you are facing a serious conflict, make a checkmark in the right column of any of the symptoms you can observe in your workplace.

Indicators:

1. There has been an increase in the absenteeism over the last year (vacation time, illness, sick leave, or other similar reasons).

2. Interpersonal relations are tainted with distrust.

3. A greater number of personnel frequently express their dissatisfaction.

4. The office climate is tense and work progresses painstakingly.

5. Performance and output have decreased.

6. You are observing an immobilization of your personnel: disinterest, detachment even from those employees who are usually very engaged.

7. Your team meetings are less and less fruitful: Some personnel arrive late or not at all. Sometimes, meetings are delayed or rescheduled because of absenteeism or an unprepared agenda.

8. It is difficult to agree on team decisions at a meeting. Sometimes important decisions are postponed, other times the process is sabotaged.

9. If the team does agree on a decision during a meeting, several members will contest their agreement or disregard the decision.

10. Personal communication is characterized by distrust and unspoken words.

11. Most people express their unmet needs or expectations through a third party, resulting in unnecessary tension.

12. Information is used as a source of power. Information is learned to possibly harm colleagues.

13. Gossip is the primary form of communication. Your team members would rather further spread the rumor than try to learn the actual facts.

14. Certain people are working with a hidden agenda.

15. The team is working without a common goal.

16. The team mentality is "everyone for himself/herself."

17. You have difficulty managing your team. You feel as though you are managing many individuals rather than one unit.

18. Your team is divided into clans that are constantly opposed; this has adverse effects.

19. Your team members are complaining that they do not really understand their specific roles. Each has his or her own idea as to what a colleague should be doing or not doing, but no one communicates their expectations of the other.

20. A large majority of the team relies on the managers and others in charge to resolve disputes.

If you checked between 1 and 9 responses, then your team is experiencing significant relationship difficulties, but there is a strong chance that the conflict can be resolved. The context in which you are situated, the will of those involved, and your leadership are all factors that can favor the resolution of your conflict and the dissipation of any unease among colleagues.

If you checked 10 or more responses, your situation is alarming. This conflict has become an unavoidable reality in your workplace and disturbs every one of your team members. Your team's efficiency and output are diminished. Because dissension has reigned for a long time, your team now challenges your leadership, which limits your actions. Several of your team members have lost faith in your ability to resolve this conflict.

Those two exercises had the same goal: to help you develop your ability to observe your team.

If you wish to further your understanding of the dynamics of conflict, I encourage you to learn each of the five stages presented in this book. By doing this, you will also find the answers to five questions that managers often ask themselves:

1. How can we create conditions that favor trust and respect and foster a healthy work environment?

2. How can we distinguish an interpersonal conflict from a team conflict?

3. How can we decelerate or stop the progression of frustrations that cause clans to form?

4. How can we provide effective support during a conflict and also maintain our leadership?

5. How can we lead a diverse team toward constructive goals?

If you have an overview of your current situation, you can effectively deploy the appropriate strategies to resolve the conflict and prevent it from producing undesirable *side effects*. For example, if the conflict you are dealing with is at the stage of forming clans and lasts for a while (a year or more), it is recommended that you contact human resources or a specialist or external coach. We can only improve the work environment through a systematic intervention involving all concerned parties. Trust me; I have seen the negative impact of certain actions that had the most honorable intentions. It is important to recognize your own limits at any time and take the right actions.

Conflict is born between people in a certain context or a certain environment at a particular time. The three elements interact and influence each other. I presented a timeline of conflict by describing the stages. Now we will discuss how individual differences (age, needs, expectations, values, life experience) can contribute to the emergence of conflict.

Does your team resemble that of the Lilly?

The experience that the crew members of the *Lilly* had is comparable to the experience of certain work teams. Several factors are similar to those in the workplace. For example, you can think of the simultaneous presence of the newer generation and the baby boomers. Their different perceptions of work can cause friction and differences in opinion. You can also think of the numerous mergers of private companies that have recently occurred, or the reorganization of civil service under a new administration, that can result in a tense climate when various workplace cultures clash. Where unlike needs exist without a feeling of unity and belonging, conflict gains strength. This is exactly what happened to the crew and passengers of the *Lilly*. Allow me to introduce you to the eight occupants:

- John, the captain

- Valerie, the hostess on board

- Marie, invited guest and friend of Valerie's

- Guy and Sylvie, a couple and paying passengers

- Me, Ghislaine, a paying passenger

- Maxime, an invited guest

- Stephane, a guest and the captain's nephew

The description of this crew and the character traits of its members reveal insight into the dynamics of relationships. These strangely resemble the dynamics of the conflicts I observed in the organizational field. Does your team resemble that of the *Lilly?*

Captain John, the typical laissez-faire leader

At 35 years old, Captain John has 20 years of sailing under his belt. His experiences are enviable. His leadership is founded in his "know-how" technique. Young at heart, he has an optimistic nature. His weakness: He fears conflict and is not very skilled in managing people.

In Business

We often encounter this type of manager, promoted because of his or her technical expertise. They are proficient at their jobs, but no one has taught them how to lead a team through changes, tension and interpersonal problems. Because they feel unable to handle conflict, they have the tendency to ignore or avoid it.

Valerie, the prima donna hostess

Having just celebrated her 17th birthday, Valerie assumed the hostess position during her summer holidays. Very reserved and hardly smiling, Valerie has an air of self-importance. Her parents asked the captain to offer her a summer job, and so he hired her as the "hostess"— a role commonly filled by a steward—aboard his sailboat. Valerie is responsible for preparing meals, but her culinary skills fall short.

In Business

Do you have any "spoiled brats" within your company? Because they are constantly striving to satisfy their own needs, these team members are individualists. The word *team* does not appear to be a part of their vocabulary. Or, do you have team members who have a privileged relationship with management or family ties with the decision-makers of your organization? These individuals may benefit from their special "support system," and this can lead to colleagues' uneasiness. It is important to take these situations in hand instead of pretending that they do not exist.

Marie, the volunteer

Also 17 years old, Marie is Valerie's friend and must help with her tasks. Of a reserved nature, she expresses herself effectively. She shows a desire to learn, despite her inexperience. Her influence on the team is more or less negligible.

In Business

We need these individuals as part of a team. Even though managers must devote some of their time to help guide and teach them, as well as integrate them with the team, their will outweighs their limited experience. They will become, with time and support, great team players. If we know how to maintain their sense of belonging to the group, we will profit on our investment (of time).

Guy, the ultimate realist

Somewhere in his 50s, Guy is the most experienced on board, second to Captain John. He knows how to make navigation plans, maneuver the boat, and direct the crew. He brings a sense of security to the vessel. Rather introverted, Guy is perceptive and not very talkative. He has a knack for determining a person's true nature. His experience as a manager has made him a prudent and informed team member. He is also capable of compromise. Guy is a good ally for the captain and the rest of his crew.

In Business

Experienced, mature, and competent, this type of crew member is a great mentor for someone younger or less experienced. He likes to perfect his knowledge in the hopes of sharing it with others. He is calm, rational; he is often called upon because of the objectivity he has displayed during difficult situations. Managers can only hope to have a team full of Guys!

Sylvie, the overly critical go-getter

In her mid-forties, Sylvie is the polar opposite of her spouse. Expressive, and with little restraint, Sylvie takes no prisoners when communicating her needs. She does not appreciate those who stand in the way of her needs. Impatient and frighteningly transparent, she destabilizes her teammates when she does not offend! As she does not like those who she feels are incompetent or inefficient, she has adopted a confrontational approach.

In Business

The "go-getter" brings his or her ideas to the table and helps the team evolve. The positive side: The innovative aspect of these people means they are always looking for opportunities to improve the functioning of the group; they also take the liberty to criticize weakness. Their motivation: the quest for perfection. The problem, however, is that they do not realize that they are stomping on the flowers! Unaware of the impact that their attitude and behavior have on their teammates, they are often very confrontational. Their spontaneous expression of ideas and opinions and their quickness to react make them an impulsive team member. Sometimes we have to curb their impulses to avoid unnecessary hiccups.

Ghislaine, the capable introvert

I treated myself to this voyage for my 41ˢᵗ birthday, like Sylvie and Guy, in the hopes of discovering the Greek isles and expanding my knowledge of sailing. Naturally introverted, I prefer calm and silence. My abilities to plan and organize render me impatient in front of inefficiency. With good analytical abilities (you might say this should be a given from any psychologist!), I can identify situations and people quite well. In fact, during some very turbulent times I shared my concerns with Captain John and offered to help him.

In Business

This type of team member enjoys assuming responsibility with quickness and efficiency. He needs conditions and guidelines for carrying out his tasks. As long as he feels appreciated and respected for his principles and values, he will continue to devote himself to his work and not count the hours he has sacrificed. All the parts work smoothly. You will be surprised to see an entirely different nature when you, even inadvertently, challenge his principles.

Maxime, the procrastinator

Only 17, Maxime, a free thinker, does not care much for rules or obligations. Why do today what you can put off until tomorrow? Long live procrastination! Captain John invited Maxime on board to introduce him to navigation.

In Business

It is difficult to predict what such individuals will contribute to a team. Because these workers are present in reality, but absent-minded, managers hesitate to give them responsibility. If we assign them a task, they complete it. If we ask them for nothing, they do not offer their help. But, new situations can highlight unknown strengths of this type of crew member. They are not big team players. The best quality lies in their preference for peace rather than creating dissension within a team.

Stephane, the powerful and charismatic leader

Both sensitive and sensible, Stephane is the youngest of the group at 16 years old. He demonstrates patience, courage and diplomacy. His open-mindedness toward the world and other people makes him a pleasant crew member. He can lead a team during tumultuous periods.

In Business

Managers often wish for many of these types of people in their teams. They can exert positive leadership in a work environment because they can equally act on the results they want to achieve and the quality of the climate and relations between the people they meet. They are good potential leaders. As managers, we should help them realize their potential. They are pearls among your team.

Do you have a John, Maxime, Valerie and others on your team?

In the next five chapters, the five stages of conflict will be presented in greater detail with the help of the following elements:

- My sailing tale

- Exercises

- A definition of each stage, including its symptoms and the most frequent reactions from the managers and team

- The responsibilities of the leaders and the teammates

- Tips to prevent or resolve the conflict at this stage

- An example of successful prevention or resolution of the conflict

- Tools for the prevention and resolution adapted for each of the five stages

- A summary of each stage in table format

For each of the stages presented, examples (from the sailing tale or organizational cases) illustrate the interactions and influence that play a role in the two other dimensions of conflict: people and their situations.

CHAPTER I: EXCLUSION

THE SAILING STORY

I landed at Athens' airport on a magnificent, sunny day. In a few hours, I would be boarding the *Lilly*, we'd lift anchor, and I'd finally realize my lifelong dream: voyaging for two weeks in the Aegean Sea with other sailing enthusiasts. Anxious, I gathered my bags and looked around, excited at the idea of meeting John, our soon-to-be captain, and the other crew members. Just a day earlier, John had called me in Montréal to tell me our meeting place at the airport. He had also told me: "You will be three passengers – a French couple and yourself. The crew will consist of myself and a hostess."

The adventure started quite badly! John showed up to our meeting point two hours late. While I had been waiting, all kinds of questions were bouncing around in my head. Where is he? Did he forget me? Will this voyage live up to my expectations? The more time passed, the more I doubted this whole endeavor. Had I been scammed? Finally, the captain arrived, breathless. His nonsensical excuses worried Guy, Sylvie and me. My first impression was overall negative.

Then, to get from the airport to the marina, all four of us packed into a Mini Cooper, baggage and all. You had to see it to believe it! The next two hours spent in suffocating heat and such a confined space greatly irritated Sylvie. I hoped that the *Lilly* would be more comfortable than the car that brought us to her and that the descriptions I had been given were accurate. Now I was starting to worry.

Upon our arrival at the marina, it seemed that the *Lilly* resembled an artist's drawing. Wow! But there was a slight hiccup: John's family was having lunch on our boat and it felt as if we were interrupting. On top of that, we had not met the hostess yet. "She'll surely arrive later," I told myself.

Our departure, scheduled for the next day at 8 a.m., was postponed until noon. Heading toward the Cyclades Isles, six of us left the marina: Captain John; the hostess, Valerie, and her friend Marie; the French couple, Guy and Sylvie; and myself, Ghislaine. The captain had confirmed that there would have been only five people. And now, another surprise! Captain John's nephew, Stephane, and Maxime (a seasonal steward) would be joining us for the second leg of our trip, sometime after the third day of our voyage. Eight of us would have to share the limited space on the sailboat.

Why take on all these young crew members? At first glance, it would seem that the only thing our crew had in common was the journey we were about to embark on. And, the captain never took the time to discuss our expectations and respective roles for the next few weeks. Our interests were varied; how could we meet the needs of two groups so dissimilar in age? Maybe my earlier worry was not unfounded? And, I don't think the captain realized that he created an unjust situation by allowing three people to participate in the journey for free when three of us paid full price! Well, I thought, this shouldn't concern me anyway. The opportunity to discover the Greek isles and explore little-known corners where most tourists never venture should more than satisfy my need for a vacation! After all, the more on board, the merrier!

The adjustment period

During the first couple of days on board, the crew members were acclimating to the new physical and social environment. Each claimed territory in his or her own way. It must be said that there is very little solitary time aboard a sailboat because of the constrained space and constant work. Thankfully, our itinerary scheduled a port at a different island each day and we could each enjoy a little time alone.

The first day went by relatively well. We tried to share the space we were given and took advantage of mealtimes to learn about one another. Everything progressed as you would expect in the formation of a new group: People attempted to socialize, bond, and similarities were slowly revealed.

Exercise

List the factors (behaviors, attitudes and manners) that contributed to creating a feeling of exclusion within the crew members of the *Lilly*.

_____

_____

_____

If you had been the captain, what could you have done differently in order to better welcome and unify your new crew members?

_____

_____

_____

If you had been a crew member, what would you have done to make the others aware of the misunderstandings or discomfort present during our period of introduction?

_____

_____

_____

Definition of the Exclusion Stage:

The initial interactions between the members of a team contribute to creating, in interested people, a sense that can be described as "I feel accepted by this group; I feel that I have my place in it." Those initial moments in the formation of a team (or the start of a group) significantly contribute to the foundation of a sense of belonging. Although it is always possible to regain your stride after a poor start, the fact remains that first impressions, among other factors, will affect the type of relationship that develops among the group members.

What happens when there is exclusion within a team? There is a notable unease for the people involved. If exclusion favors conflict, it will not necessarily provoke it systematically. Exclusion is created when there is an absence of satisfactory responses from other team members to the needs of integration and inclusion of new teammates.

For example, imagine that a new hire joins a current work team. She most likely will expect a colleague to invite her to lunch during her first week in the hopes of establishing a warmer relationship with her. But, she is not going to share this hope with her new colleague. When the invitation doesn't happen, she starts to believe that the colleague does not appreciate her presence, and this perception is reinforced each time she feels this colleague is distant.

Note that exclusion also can happen to a colleague who has already been part of the team for a while. An established team member may feel threatened or pushed out by a new colleague. In both cases, dissatisfied needs at this stage will reinforce the individual's perception that his environment (work or otherwise) cannot meet his needs for inclusion and a sense of belonging.

Many situations can hinder the integration and inclusion process. Think of a new hire who has not been introduced to his team, another who didn't have access to a promotion that was accessible to other members, or a new leader who let too much time elapse before meeting his team. All of those situations provoke questions and doubts. In the absence of timely and precise information, your personnel will rely on their own interpretations of the new reality they are facing.

Circumstances that contribute to exclusion

1. *Neglecting to welcome one or more new team members.* Yes, you may be aware of the importance of this slight gesture, but you fail to do so because time does not allow it.

2. *Leave team members to welcome themselves by neglecting to introduce them or not leading any team-bonding activities.*

Leaders take for granted the idea that employees will be in accordance when the leader is absent.

3. *Ignoring (intentionally or not) a new member.* In some situations, the team that has to welcome its new member is concurrently mourning the loss of a previous member. Therefore, it can be difficult for the newcomer to feel welcome.

4. *Constantly praising a new team member when he or she does not necessarily merit it.* If a manager constantly praises his new recruit, the other team members will suspect he is playing favorites, which does nothing to help the unity of a team.

5. *Remaining closed off about your new members, ignoring the recruits, distancing yourself, or adopting a defensive attitude toward them.* Maybe your comfortable situation prevents you from realizing the effect your actions have on your colleagues. But what if it were you, the newcomer?

There are many situations that can lead to the poor beginnings of working relationships. A new hire's need to quickly learn to perform his job can overshadow his desire to acquaint himself with his colleagues. It's even happened that I've forgotten to introduce myself before a speech! The client had reduced my speaking time because the day had been overbooked. Like everyone else, I needed to make the most of my shortened time but I didn't realize the effects on the quality of my professional relationships. About 10 minutes into my presentation, a participant sheepishly asked my name and profession, a legitimate question. Because I had wanted to delve right into the material of my presentation, I neglected even the most elementary aspect of speaking.

Whatever the motive, certain behaviors and actions – voluntary or not – can hinder the integration process.

The feeling of exclusion aboard the Lilly

Here is how the feeling of exclusion manifested on the sailboat.

Causes and indicators

- The first impression we gathered of Captain John. His excessive tardiness and poor welcome upon meeting his passengers at the airport instilled the feeling that he did not respect them.

- The absence of Valerie, the hostess, who was supposed to greet the passengers.

- The fact that the captain did not clearly indicate until the last minute which people (and how many) would be part of the journey.

- The restricted space in the car and the sailboat, along with limited access to certain resources.

- The perception that the *Lilly* was unprepared for the arrival of its new passengers, triggered by the presence of the captain's family members having lunch.

Simple welcoming gestures would have made a huge difference.

Responsibilities of the leader

The captain could have been more straightforward about his intentions from the beginning. He could have told us then the details of the last-minute changes. He also could have justified the presence of the young crew by explaining that he took advantage of the slower season to introduce them to sailing. He could have expressed his understanding of our different expectations and experience by indicating how he would adapt to those differences. He also could have strived to meet his crew's needs by discussing our expectations and proposing concrete plans designed to strengthen his team. With this kind of beginning, the team members would have felt that the person in charge was concerned with their needs and that integration was possible.

Responsibilities of the team members

In most situations, starting things off on the right foot is as much the responsibility of the team members as it is of the leader. In our case, the crew members could have asked, "Who is part of the team and what is each person's role?" They could have expressed their reservations about traveling with passengers who had such a disparity in age and experience, and tried to learn what each person's expectations were. Together, they could have established guidelines for living together and, in the case of the working crew, specified job duties, meanwhile ensuring that the overall needs of the group were met.

Frequent reactions

Feeling excluded can generate varied emotional responses, including retreating and ignoring or attempting to punish the person or people who are producing the exclusion.

There are other signs that may help you identify the difficulties that a team may have to deal with and overcome when trying to integrate its new members. Not satisfactorily meeting the team member's needs for inclusion causes friction and prevents the group from functioning harmoniously. The following list provides an overview of those other signs:

- One or two members are having trouble integrating with the team. Whatever the cause – differences in the individuals, different levels of expertise, inability to adapt to others – if even one member has trouble integrating with the team, it can slow down the bonding process for everyone.

- Certain members don't have an interest in merging with the team, and maintain a stubbornly individualistic work style.

- A very qualified new addition to a group can cause insecurities to surface in the existing team members. As a result, the latter may tacitly or explicitly reject the new member.

- There may a lack of initiative to promote collaboration within a team, which could generate a sense of rejection for the newcomer.

- Initially, the manager must realize that there may be a timid reception or a less-than-enthusiastic reaction from the newly united team members. This is normal at first. But if the problem persists after several months, it is important to alert the parties involved to their unwelcoming reaction and encourage them to participate more in meetings and within their teams.

Try to identify the indications of the feeling of exclusion in the following situation, which comes from a case study from an organization.

Organizational Case No. 1

A Poor Start

Two newly hired representatives are part of the same team and must share the responsibilities and representation of their territory. Because their clients are widely spread out, the team members have very little time to meet face to face. So, it is only after several months that a conflict emerges between the two. Let's examine the profiles of our representatives.

Sophie is working as a sales representative for the first time. Although she knows her environment well, having worked in a related field, she still needs to learn her new job. She is organized, methodical and a perfectionist. She hopes to make a good impression on her new employer.

Melanie previously worked for a competitor and has 10 years of experience as a sales representative. She is independent and doesn't like to be controlled; however, she does like to influence others. According to her, she manages to attain the objectives of her company and meet deadlines by prioritizing.

The uneasiness starts

Sophie was the first one hired, around early fall. Eight months later, she is promoted to sales representative, just as she'd hoped. The team members she originally worked with had been assigned to a different position a few months later. Melanie is hired in June. The fiscal year is already in progress, projects have been planned, and vacations are approaching. Sophie presents the current projects to Melanie. They begin to discuss the other projects that must be completed by the end of the year. Melanie shares some of her ideas but doesn't feel as though her new colleague is really interested. She tells Sophie her strengths and previous accomplishments. Concerned with delays and unsure of her priorities, Sophie ends the discussion and postpones it until she returns from her holidays.

Fall arrives, and the discussion has still not taken place. The two women's immediate supervisor asks that they present him with a plan of their priorities, a report of their client development, and the resulting budget they've created. The two have different ideas and disagree on how to proceed. Melanie, once more, doesn't feel that her colleague welcomes her suggestions. The communication disintegrates and hurtful words are exchanged during a meeting. This is the first incident between them and they abruptly end their meeting.

Two months later, Melanie attempts to converse with her colleague in the hopes of easing the tension. Because she doesn't like conflict, she feels uneasy in her current situation. The discussion quickly reaches an impasse. The two part ways feeling hurt and now avoid each other at work. When the supervisor learns that they are no longer talking to each other, he is surprised at how quickly their professional relationship has deteriorated to this point.

Your analysis

What are the indicators of the uneasiness?

_____

_____

_____

The importance of recognizing the need for inclusion

Promoting successful integration is certainly an important step when a new team is formed or a new member added to an existing team. In this respect, I recall a professional experience where I had assumed a position of leadership in organizational development for a defined period of time. From my arrival, I expressed my need to meet my supervisor to establish my objectives in the position that had just been created for me. After three weeks, I didn't get to meet with my superior and so I had to function with my own perception of my role, not receiving any clarification on my duties or expectations from my new boss.

When basic needs aren't met, it's likely that the person will manifest his or her dissatisfaction. However, there are numerous needs (some, admittedly, are more difficult to identify than others) not recognized in a professional environment. The simple act of recognizing the legitimacy of human needs, rather than trivializing them, demonstrates a constructive attitude. Among employees' common needs, we should mention the need to belong, to work in a secure environment or one conducive to reaching their full potential, to feel respected, valued and appreciated for their knowledge, talents, and contribution to the team…and so on.

Managers can't guarantee that all of their employees' needs will be met. However, when the realistic needs are expressed and not satisfied, the buildup inevitably leads to frustration. Making an effort to recognize employees' needs and attempting to meet them in a way that is compatible with the values and culture of your organization are proactive ways to encourage inclusion, a necessary step in building team morale.

Tips to prevent exclusion

Here is some advice for the leader and team members aimed at cultivating the feeling of inclusion.

Advice for the leader

The leader has a key role in ensuring the integration of his personnel.

- *Welcome your new team members.* This seems to be a given. But, many people don't make an effort to shake a new employee's hand. It's more difficult to guarantee the cohesion of a team if we neglect the initial welcoming gesture, which reinforces team spirit and contributes to the feeling of belonging.

- *Reserve time to greet and integrate your new team members.* I saw the supervisor of a small business repeat this same mistake several times. He had hired a key person, whom he intended to work closely with over time. But, this recruit often had to take over the supervisor's post during business trips that lasted as long as three weeks. Is it necessary to specify that the timing to integrate this new hire was not ideal?

- *Be available at all times.* I can attest that, as managers, you don't have much time to spare and that you are overworked and too often occupied with meetings that are more or less important. Know to make the right choice and establish your priorities. After all, the faster your new hire is acclimated and able to fully fulfill her job duties, the faster you can delegate tasks and reduce your workload. You can clearly indicate that you are available by providing several ways for your employees to contact you (e-mail, voicemail, etc.) when you're away from the office.

- *Promote positive interactions and activities to encourage contact as soon as possible.* Why not take advantage of the next meeting and devote an hour to promote team-bonding? You can do this with humor. For example, you can refer to a quality, a passion, an interest, or even joke about an embarrassing situation that happened to you. This can enhance collaboration within a team working on a project.

- *Form interchangeable "sub-teams."* By creating well-trained, interchangeable "sub-teams" for precise projects or common dossiers, you will better promote the team's cohesion by encouraging collaboration.

- *Clearly define team members' roles and specify why each person is important within the group.* Simply reading job descriptions is not the best way to develop a common understanding of each person's roles and responsibilities. An activity where each member presents his perception of his responsibilities, followed by a team discussion leading to a consensus, is the best way to develop understanding and a common vision. This can help to prevent situations in which, for fear of refusal or rejection, team members hesitate to ask for cooperation or help from their colleagues.

- *Establish the rules from the beginning: respect, trust cooperation...and specify how they are applied.* The manager instills the climate he desires within his team through his own actions and behavior. If he makes it clear, for example, that he won't tolerate a lack of respect between colleagues, those altercations are less likely to happen. But be careful! The person in charge must act as a role model and his behavior must be congruent with his words and his vision.

- *Reinforce open-mindedness toward others.* Nothing is easier than applying operant conditioning techniques by providing positive feedback on attitudes and behaviors you wish to encourage or maintain. For example, if during a meeting a colleague adopts an open-minded attitude and offers his collaboration, the supervisor can reinforce that by saying, "I'm very happy that Peter offered to help his new colleague. I'm sure that others will do the same when the opportunity lends itself." These methods are just as efficient in adults as they are in children!

- *Specify your expectations and your limits.* You aren't psychic and you can't guess everyone's expectations. It's the responsibility of each member to express his needs and find ways to meet them. The manager should make his team members understand that the satisfaction of their needs relies most on their desire to persevere until they are met. If faced with unrealistic demands or expectations, the manager should insist that his personal limits and professional constraints are respected, the same limits to which he must adhere.

Advice for the team

The following attitudes should be reinforced and maintained within the members of your team.

- *Take the time to know your colleagues and employees.* Casually invite them to have a coffee or lunch. But, don't invite them all at once! It's much harder to get to know someone if an imposing group is present.

- *Appreciate your coworkers' good qualities, or, if applicable, try to discover them.* Instead of perceiving a new hire as a threat, think of him or her as an ally. After all, individual differences are what complete a team and enable it to better cope with challenges.

- *Be aware of your own strengths and limits.* Communication and teamwork are easier to establish if you know the extent of your strengths and recognize your limits.

- *Avoid judging your colleagues solely on first impressions.* Judging a person can create distrust, isn't conducive to a good work environment, and can make it difficult to establish honest and effective communication.

- *Take the initiative concerning your professional relationships and clearly state your expectations, needs and contributions.* As I mentioned in the section for the leader, clearly expressing your needs can decrease frustration. You must take responsibility for your needs and, if someone refuses to meet them, you will have a clearer picture of the reasoning behind it. As a result, you'll be less likely to immediately attribute it to malicious intent.

- *Invest yourself in your work environment; participate in team activities and other social and networking events.* The feeling of belonging can be created outside of the work environment through social activities with your team members.

An example successful inclusion: multidisciplinary teams

As part of a strategy to conquer new markets that will develop over the next five years, our model company, GVC, decided to implement a sales structure that utilizes a cross-marketing approach. As a result, GVC's sales team will be restructured for different markets in order to offer consumers the entire range of products and services of the company, rather than structured to promote only a certain product. In order to achieve this, GVC created multidisciplinary teams made up of sales personnel, customer service representatives, production employees, and estimators; all of these individuals are in different regions from one another. The formation of these new teams has led to important changes with respect to how employees define their roles and how they work together. In collaboration with the head of human resources, we designed team-building activities that were presented to each new team. The goal was to support the team leaders during these changes. The workshop was intended to:

- Develop a common understanding of the company's new vision.

- Establish everyone's roles and contributions in the organizational structure.

- Familiarize the team members and focus on individual assessments using Myers-Briggs Type Indicator (MBTI) [1].

The results were very positive. For every newly formed team, members were able to:

- Learn one another's strengths and weaknesses.

- Participate in developing a team plan specifying the function of each: short-term and intermediate goals, values, expected contributions from each person, organizing meetings.

- Quickly establish communication between employees that allows them to work efficiently and attain their objectives.

Prevention tools adapted for this stage

If you're wondering what to do to favor inclusion when forming new work teams or groups for a project, here are some ideas:

- *Activities designed to welcome and integrate.* All activities that can help to acquaint and integrate new employees and familiarize them with their new work environment, along with determining resources and the tools available for team members. A good example of that is a teambuilding session.

- *Clarification of roles and responsibilities.* Understanding the contribution of team members and establishing a consensus for team members' roles is certainly an efficient strategy in maximizing everyone's potential. If you conduct such an activity, you'll be surprised at the questions and revelations arising, even if the colleagues have known one another for years.

- *Activities that favor teamwork, communication, and understanding one another's differences.* Several consultants and training companies offer these sorts of activities. Know how to identify the ones that meet your needs or ask a professional to assist you in needs assessment.

- *Coaching for managers.* If the leadership of the team isn't your biggest strength, there's no shame in seeking help from a person who can support you while you develop this skill. Team-management and conflict-management skills can be developed!

Summary

Stage 1: Exclusion

The absence of willingness to include an individual, leader, or a sub-group within a team.

	Symptoms/Indicators Present	Tools and Techniques to Prevent Exclusion	Indicators of Improvement
Type of Energy	• Unfocused energy	–	• Productive energy
Climate	• Embarrassment, shyness	–	• A welcoming climate
Communication	• Unease caused by the presence of certain people	• Provide integrating activities: presentations, exercises that encourage mingling with others	• Team members are more relaxed during discussions
Interpersonal Relations	• Difficult for a team member to integrate himself	• Favor the establishing of relationships among coworkers – create diverse yet interchangeable "sub-teams"	• An absence or decrease in members' comparing themselves with their peers, a lack of jealousy and envious
Work Teams	• Poor participation during meetings	• Specify each person's roles and responsibilities	• Members of your team form bonds, a good rapport, and recognize their contributions
Attitudes	• A defensive attitude; "Waiting for the other to take the first step"	• Reinforce an open-minded attitude	• Sensing a desire for teamwork
Needs	• Inclusion, an individual's desire to "fit in"	• Provide training for the managers concerning teamwork, a team's stages of evolution, managing meetings	• No more disputes for space, each member has his or her own "three feet"

Exclusion ← → Inclusion

Exclusion ← → Inclusion

Frequent Reactions

From Team Members	From Leaders
Failing to recognize the benefit of a team and maintaining an individualistic working style	Not paying attention to the integration needs of a team
Ignoring a new member or not extending any welcome	Unclear roles – not taking the time to clarify each member's role within a team
Tacitly or explicitly rejecting a teammate	Not clarifying his or her expectations toward the team
Opting for a defensive attitude upon the arrival of a new teammate (colleague, leader or sub-group)	Not reacting to the first signs of the stage of exclusion
Postponing a necessary collaboration of team members	

CHAPTER 2: CONFRONTATION

THE SAILING STORY

The second day of our journey was the most demanding: 55 nautical miles before our next stop at an island, Serifos, a distance represented by 11 hours of navigation! A long journey awaited us, yet we started to sail only at 10:45 a.m. The constant rolling of the boat produced some undesirable effects: Marie and I had been seasick since the boat had lifted anchor.

At sea, you must be able to satisfy the basic needs for food, sleep and warmth. In other words, to eat, sleep and dress accordingly. The sun and its sweltering heat can equally cause physical exhaustion. So, if we don't take care to meet our physical needs, we diminish our essential resources; and in the event that one of the crew becomes sick, that person becomes a burden for the rest of the team.

The expression of different needs

Those who are familiar with sailing know that everyone must adhere to certain rules that keep in mind the needs of the entire crew. Respect for others and their space is crucial for the team to live harmoniously in a habitat where overcrowding is such an issue.

Unfortunately, certain rules were not respected, especially those concerning departure times, mealtimes, food purchases and bedtimes. The annoyances multiplied. The meals were neither being prepared nor served at regular times; therefore, our need to be fed was not respected. The younger members of our group weren't early risers and would stay up late chatting on the deck, preventing the rest of us from falling asleep. Bottled water, which was to be distributed at will, was not offered to everyone. For breakfast, many times the passengers needed to fetch bread or other basics because the hostess had not prepared the meal in advance.

Those numerous small irritants were recorded on our emotional meters – especially as our needs weren't met. Sylvie, very annoyed by these shortcomings, begins to confide in me. Our discussions focused more on our unmet needs and complaints rather than the pleasure that our cruise brings us.

In a very polite way, Sylvie and I shared our discontent with the rest of the crew. Sylvie initially presented some suggestions concerning our food to our hostess, Valerie. But, realizing her suggestions were not taken seriously, Sylvie adopted a more aggressive tone and demanded that her needs be met. I raised the problems of the noise after 11 p.m. and the lack of bottled water. We had a right to a hearing of our needs and suggestions.

From the beginning, I felt the tension rise within our team. Our differences of opinion about how to live while on board infiltrated our discussions. The relationship between Valerie and Sylvie was strained, as neither one seemed open to a compromise. On one hand, Sylvie demands respect: "If Valerie took into consideration my needs, there wouldn't be a problem and our voyage would be more pleasant." On the other hand, Valerie confides in her friend Marie, "If Sylvie stopped berating me and making offensive remarks, I wouldn't lose face in front of everyone."

Not noticing a change in Valerie's behavior, Sylvie openly complained in front of the captain about her attitude and unprofessional manner. Because of those unpleasant comments, Valerie took a defensive attitude, while Sylvie, still feeling that her needs were not being considered, became more and more unwavering. The two confront each other more frequently as their discontent progresses.

The next evening, the captain attempted a diversion by inviting us to dine at a taverna on the island. We were offered a modest supper of diverse Greek dishes. It was the first full meal we had eaten together since our departure from the marina, and offered a release of the tension within the crew of the *Lilly*, especially as Valerie was not subject to Sylvie's criticisms. Marie and I were grateful for a meal on land as we got a break from our ever-present seasickness. I was suffering from fatigue. Was it due to hunger, thirst, seasickness, a lack of sleep, or the tension on board? I am almost certain that this last reason was a significant cause of my malaise.

Exercise

List, from the sailing story, all the situations where our needs were not met, which led to confrontation between certain members of the crew.

_____

_____

_____

If you had been the captain, what would you have done to manage this stage of confrontation?

_____

_____

_____

If you had been a crew member, what would you have done to facilitate the expression and satisfaction of everyone's varying needs?

_____

_____

_____

Definition of the Confrontation Stage

The Confrontation Stage results from a poor expression of needs and differences. There is a "collision" of needs, values and interests, which ultimately incites friction.

The confrontation took place when people had an interdependent relationship (such as working together or being part of the same team), when they had to share the same resources or environment, and when they expressed their different needs, expectations and values, but failed to respectfully listen to the others and reach an agreement. If the people involved cannot reach a solution that meets their needs, there is a risk for conflicted relationship and considerable friction.

In a work environment where the expression of differences is not tolerated, or team members view those differences as difficulties to overcome, an eventual intensification of those needs is predictable.

There will be confrontation if, in a context where not all needs can be met, a person demands his or hers be met at the expense of colleague's needs. According to the *Oxford Dictionary*, "to confront" means to "oppose, as in hostility or a competition."

In dialogue that exhibits respect and openness, it's beneficial to confront needs. In the absence of those conditions, confrontation can lead to awkwardness, offensive statements, and debates that will invariably progress to the next stage – the intensification of conflict.

It is incorrect to believe that unmet needs will simply disappear with time. This is the second misconception, after "time heals all wounds," that most people need to drop.

Circumstances contributing to confrontation

1. *Judging others because of their idiosyncrasies and differences without trying to understand them.* I often say, "What a person cannot understand, he interprets and judges." Differences can be scary, but they help us grow on a personal level.

2. *Always thinking that others are wrong and that you are right.* If you're always out to prove that you are right, don't be surprised when others start to avoid you. There is a much more effective way to succeed: Put your influence to work! But, you can only influence the position of your colleagues if you have established a trusting relationship.

3. *Believing that your needs are more important than those of the team.* If this message is often conveyed in your attitude, you are setting yourself up for confrontation.

4. *Denying people's individual differences, which is akin to putting everyone in the same mold.* Most people don't like being treated in this manner.

5. *Avoiding discussions about differences in opinion.* While the avoidance strategy may be suitable in some situations, it won't solve any problems. It's as if you are obligating the people who disagree to pretend to get along. After some time, the situation becomes stifling.

6. *Accumulating unsaid words.* Unfortunately, many still believe – wrongly – that ignoring perceived wrongdoings would still bring change, that someone will intervene. Unsaid words are common in situations of conflict and certainly don't contribute to reestablishing a pleasant climate.

7. *Overvaluing the team's "superstar."* Wanting to reinforce the skills of an exceptionally qualified member, the leader presents him or her as an example. But, if a manager constantly praises the same person, he is setting up the team for unhealthy competition.

8. *Not intervening as a manager during the confrontation stage.* This endorses a passive approach to the resolution of conflicts.

Confrontation aboard the Lilly

Let's see how the Confrontation Stage manifested itself on the sailboat.

Causes and indicators

- The delay in leaving each morning.

- The lack of respect for the group's physical needs, such as the problems regarding the mealtimes and the food served, bedtimes, and the spotty availability of bottled water.

- The fact that the hostess didn't complete her tasks; she neglected to prepare adequate courses and make the necessary arrangements to serve the meals at a reasonable time.

- The different needs of the two sub-groups (the older passengers and younger crew) and a failure to communicate and understand each other.

- The fact that the needs of the two groups were conflicting. The paying passengers wanted to enjoy the cruise and receive what was promised to them, whereas the young crew members favored immediate pleasure.

- A lack of leadership from the captain, who should have set rules and facilitated communication between Sylvie and Valerie.

Responsibilities of the leader

The captain should have led a constructive discussion about the team's needs. During the discussion, he could have reiterated the need for respect among the crew and established general rules. Given the complaints against the hostess, he could have encouraged her to create different menus, helped her in fulfilling her duties, or even asked the other members of the crew for help. After all, the captain is responsible for the atmosphere on his boat and he needs to ensure that the tasks he delegates to his crew are completed.

Responsibilities of the team

Considering the heavy climate and disagreements they'd experienced, our crew could have:

- Requested a group discussion in order to set rules and establish the roles and responsibilities of each person while ensuring that both individual and group needs were met within the team.

- Put an end to the quarrels between Sylvie and Valerie and suggested new menu options.

- Avoided pointless confrontations and asked the captain to clarify his expectations for his crew and the values to be respected.

Some common reactions

If we refuse to listen to someone who is expressing a need, or fail to recognize the person, the individual can manifest his or her discontent by:

- Refusing to express his or her needs from then on, which can lead to the neglect of those needs.

- Denying the emerging conflict, which often involves minimizing or trivializing the problem.

- Avoiding situations where someone may provoke a confrontation.

- Accumulating frustration and unspoken words.

- Confronting people who have different opinions or different ways of doing things.

- Having a contradictory attitude or the will to win at all costs.

- Hoping (often unrealistically) that the leader or person responsible will find an immediate solution to his unsatisfied needs.

- Affirming his needs in a positive way and taking responsibility for his own satisfaction … a rather uncommon reaction!

Now, try to identify the indicators that foreshadowed the conflict between the members of the team in the following organizational case.

Organizational Case No. 2

Two Generations Conflict

A human resources team is experiencing some difficulties in its operation. The person in charge, Ginette, consults an external coach to try to get through the impasse. Consisting of professionals and administrative personnel, the human resources team has different but complementary objectives among its members. The professionals offer the leaders support in managing their human capital. They're young, dynamic, full of new ideas, but, for the most part, have little work experience. Those from administrative personnel – one sub-group responsible for the staff, one responsible for payroll, and one responsible for benefits – have more experience in the field, and comply with and respect company policies. They're more traditional in respect to their role as "guardians" of those policies. Preferring clearly defined procedure, they expect rules to be followed and fair leadership.

Marc has worked as a consultant for this organization for nearly a year. His colleagues have noticed that he often gives inaccurate information to his clients. At other moments, to hide his incompetence, he fails to meet his clients' requests or simply does not comply. As a result, his requests end up going to his colleague Frank, although they don't fall within his area of expertise. On several occasions, Frank has told his supervisor, Ginette, about the situation and she has told him to be patient and that she will intervene. In the meantime, Ginette invites Frank to respond to all of Marc's client requests.

While this situation continues unfairly, the human resources team is dealing with an important transition. The company's growth requires the team to define the services offered and organize the labor. Everyone's workload increases, and so the conflicts multiply. Although the administrative personnel invest themselves into their tasks and even work overtime (for which only some members are compensated), the professionals refuse to work more than the standard 40 hours per week. Their personal lives are just as important to them as their professional ones, and if they have to work overtime, they want to be compensated or have extended vacations. The debate becomes particularly heated when it comes to defining the rules that must apply to both groups.

Not knowing how to approach this delicate subject, Ginette postpones her answer, hoping to gain some time to think. Meanwhile, the team members start complaining about the lack of collaboration among colleagues when it comes to expediting common files. The conflict builds and is bound to explode if nothing is done to clear up the situation and establish specific rules.

Your analysis

What factors further exacerbated the conflict?

_____

_____

_____

The importance of managing divergent needs

Our needs are a reflection of our values. For example, certain workers of the baby boomer generation need a sense of belonging within their work organization. They often attach value to their loyalty toward their employers, something not as common among the newer generations that have seen numerous layoffs and restructuring during the '90s. Respect of their personal values (a balance between work and leisure, or satisfying their needs) ranks highly on their list of organizational values.

In summary, the cohabitation of three or more generations, in the workplace can generate multiple conflicts. Because it's difficult to change others' values, the rules of an organization must take into consideration everyone's needs. Our human resources case study is quite common. How many working groups are going through the same malaise? If the approach the team takes strives to reconcile differences rather than disregard them, the results will be much more eloquent.

In the example presented here, the factors that contributed to the unproductive conflicts are:

1. The inequity that resulted from one team member not fulfilling all of his duties.

2. The existence of unjust rules concerning compensation for overtime. The professionals benefit from a different treatment than that given to the administrative professionals.

3. The expression of differences between the members and the lack of intervention by the manager.

4. The delayed intervention by the manager after the team confronted her. Her procrastination allowed a tense and unpleasant climate to develop.

Responsibilities of the leader

Even though employees determine the quality of their work environment by their interactions with their colleagues, managers are still responsible for the atmosphere within their workplace. By not intervening appropriately when a team member fails to accomplish his tasks and leaving the other colleagues to pick up the pieces, the manager creates a situation marked by inequity. And, if such a situation isn't resolved, it inevitably leads to overt confrontation among the colleagues. Equality is a prominent value and even the perception of inequality can create heated debates.

In the case of our human resources team, the leader was trying to micromanage the situation. By wanting to respect the needs of the sub-groups and endorsing different overtime payment policies, she created a controversial situation. Because she adopted differing, more flexible rules, for her team, Ginette had to deal with several outstanding demands; in fact, certain members of the team demanded she focus on their individual needs rather than those of the team. There is a price to pay when choosing Ginette's approach: Demands of this nature will multiply and they will be the source of much debate.

In fact, these difficulties emerged because the team was mid-restructuring, a circumstance in which it's crucial to reexamine the way things are being done and to make sure that the rules fit the new context.

It is important to ensure that different opinions are expressed respectfully and with one goal in mind: finding a solution that will meet the new needs. A difficult task, you say? Yes, but a fruitful one. Skipping this very important step will only lead to more problems. And, if the conflict explodes, the resources and time that will be required will be twofold. It's your choice to decide whether you want to define your team's needs during a calm time rather than during a crisis.

The responsibilities of the team

It's up to each team member to make his or her needs and expectations known in order to optimize the chances of having them met. But, how many people have trouble expressing them clearly during a conflict? Too often, without even having tried to clearly state their needs, people expect others to ensure their satisfaction. Choosing this route relieves people of responsibility for their own satisfaction and confines them to the role of victim. **Everyone has the power to choose.** This is the fundamental theme of Annie Marquier's book *The Power of Choice* (title translated from French).

Tips to prevent confrontation

Advice for the leader

Encourage the expression of individual needs. Easier said than done! Encouraging the expression of their differences doesn't imply that you are obligated to accept everyone's viewpoints or respond to their divergent needs. After this exercise, you'll have to redirect the discussion toward the common needs of the team. This is a good way to legitimize everyone's needs without suppressing anyone, yet capitalizing on the situation by finding new solutions.

Lead with equality, avoid taking sides. Managing human capital has greatly evolved. Because professional teams today are made up of individuals spanning different generations, certain issues arise as a result. For example, workers are increasingly demanding more flexible work schedules. We make no mistake when acquiescing to these requests. But, we are making a mistake when meeting demands that don't coincide with the needs of the organization. A just but flexible management takes into account both collective and individual needs.

Recognize each of your team members' potential. Yes! The players who are underused or not allowed the chance to showcase their talents will eventually worry that their personal needs aren't being satisfied. It is known that a person who feels valued at work is less inclined to focus on negligible inequalities or to compare himself with colleagues. Team-bonding activities are notably effective in exposing the diverse potentials and opinions on individual differences.[2]

Rely on your team's compatibility. On this subject, my point of view is simple enough. If you have a team that is colored orange, they will produce excellent orange results. But, when your clients ask you for blue results, you won't be able to produce them. In fact, you must utilize the full potential of each of your teammates, and exploit it to reach the objectives of the team. By acknowledging differences and relying on your team's interdependence to find innovative ways of completing tasks, you'll transform the confrontation stage into a constructive one, crucial for the evolution of your team.

Intervene quickly when a conflict arises between two people. An excellent way to do this is to offer your support and help to the people involved in the conflict. Rather than letting them search for a solution or compromise alone, offer them your assistance as a mediator or, if not comfortable with this role, get a coach to help you. Your task will be less arduous, as you won't need to decide who is making a more reasonable demand. You'll be guiding the two parties while they look for solutions that suit both of them.

Advice for the team

- *Stop comparing yourself with others!* You've heard the expression "The grass is always greener on the other side." If you start to list your own advantages and benefits, will it reestablish certain equilibrium?

- *Preoccupy yourself with your work climate.* It rests on all colleagues to maintain the quality of their professional relationships. Don't let any disagreement or discomfort linger. Remember: "He who doesn't express himself only impacts himself." In other words, keeping your dissatisfaction to yourself only serves to anchor it further.

- *Confront irresponsible colleagues.* If colleagues reach a disagreement, invite them to discuss and attempt a solution. Don't listen passively; instead, redirect them toward their responsibilities. If colleagues have addressed you about the same matter regarding another colleague more than three times in the hopes that you will rectify the matter, invite them to pursue their own unsatisfied needs. After all, if they refuse to intervene in this supposedly frustrating situation, maybe their needs are not so important to them after all.

An example of success: Strengthening the human resources team

In the previous example, we tried resolving the problem by working on strengthening the team. Confronting the opposing needs of the two sub-groups was the focus of the activity. After an exercise on the appreciation of differences as defined through the Myers-Briggs Type Indicator (openness to differences other than age), the team members were invited to devise their expectations in terms of their respective areas. We have noted four sub-groups: personnel responsible for the staff, personnel responsible for payroll, personnel responsible for benefits, and finally, more general knowledge professionals. Each of these sub-groups was asked to convey the expectations they had with respect to the other sub-groups.

Joining the team members with similar roles helped to break down the barriers of communication between the administrative personnel and the professionals and prevented the team from dividing itself into two factions. By formulating a game plan, the teammates were able to use different means to meet the diverse needs of the team. They were:

- A brief meeting for all personnel at the beginning of each week with the objective of sharing news.

- A monthly meeting between the professionals to discuss the evolution of projects and current dockets, and, if necessary, to assist one another.

- A quarterly meeting for the entire team to review objectives, recognize achievements, determine which actions are necessary to attain the new goals, and, finally, to reinforce the feeling of belonging to a team.

And what happened to Marc, who had trouble integrating with his team and efficiently completing his duties? The strengthening of the team made him aware that his professional capacities didn't meet the needs of the organization (and vice-versa). He announced his departure a few days after the activity.

As for Ginette and her style of leadership, she realized that by trying to please everyone (in other words, showing herself as incapable of refusing certain demands), she often made decisions that led to an unfair work environment that provoked conflict within her team. The problem of overtime hours was resolved by taking into account each post and its requirements, rather than the personal needs of the employee.

A good lesson in leadership can be retained: **Don't believe that by acquiescing to all of your employees' demands you will make everyone happy.** At first, the results of this management style seem encouraging, but in the long run, you contribute to a chaotic and frustrating situation.

Prevention tools adapted for this stage

- If you're wondering what you can particularly do to prevent confrontation, here are suggestions:

- *Lead a discussion on how to properly express differences and reach a consensus.* Admit that a team is undergoing difficulties related to its operations. Many complain about the lack of transparency when it comes to scheduling, holidays and managing the replacements. The manager calls for a meeting where team members are invited to propose their rules of operations. After a few hours of animated discussion, they finally reach a consensus and the majority of them are surprised at the results of this meeting.

- *Hold team-building sessions.* This type of intervention makes it possible to meet a team's needs for cohesion and efficiency. Consolidating a team can take many forms, depending on the objectives you're striving for. Having conducted these types of activities several times in different situations, I can attest to their effectiveness in preventing or defusing conflicts.

Offer awareness workshops on:

- Maintaining a healthy work environment.

- Effective communication.

- Collaborating and teamwork.

- Effective management of meetings.

- Preventing conflict.

Although the objective of these workshops is not to delve deeply into the dynamics of relationships, they help prevent conflicts and allow the participants to examine and perfect the way they manage their professional relationships.

Summary

Stage 2: Confrontation

Ineffective expression of needs and differences. "Collision" of needs, values, and interests, which leads to friction.

	Symptoms/Indicators Present	Tips and Techniques to Prevent Confrontation	Signs of Improvement
Energy Type	• Confrontational energy	—	• Harmonious energy
Climate	• Tense climate	—	• Amiable climate
Communication	• The expression of different ideas and opinions creates tension and friction	• Promote the expression of differences in an open and trusting climate	• Team members feel at ease when expressing their differences and do so without fear of being threatened
Interpersonal Relationships	• Judgments are made based on differences	• Recognize the legitimacy of the differences in needs, values, and ideas	• Team members explore and respect their individual differences
Work Teams	• It is difficult for the team to reach an agreement	• When ideas clash, direct the discussion towards a favorable solution	• Decisions are made by consensus: Each team member has the chance to speak his or her mind and influence the final choice
Attitudes	• Close-minded attitude toward those with different values and needs	• Maintain the concept that the expression and acceptance of different ideas leads to ingenious solutions	• Team members take pleasure in talking to one another and discovering new possibilities
Needs	• Distinct	• Lead team-strengthening activities: communication exercises, team cooperation • Provide workshops that focus on creating a healthy work climate, communication, teamwork, and conflict prevention and resolution	• The leader doesn't fear spirited meetings that focus on controversial topics

Confrontation ←——————→ Acceptance of differences

Frequent Reactions

From the Team Members	From the Leader
A refusal to express ideas and needs to the point of abandoning them altogether	Incorrectly believing that the group can resolve problems on its own
Denying that a conflicting situation is emerging	Attributing the difficulties to a lack of compatibility
Fleeing or avoiding situations	Not responding to and fleeing conflicting situations
Accumulating unspoken words and frustrations	
Provoking confrontation for the purpose of creating controversy	
Waiting for a reaction from the leader	
Positively affirming his needs, but not at the expense of others	

CHAPTER 3: THE FORMATION OF FACTIONS

THE SAILING STORY

Day 3: We planned our departure for 10:30 a.m. We made a quick stop at Sifnos, an island where we had time for a refreshing swim. Our lunch was substantial enough: eggs and salami. About 7:30 p.m. we arrived at Folegandros, once again starving and exhausted.

On the way, Sylvie and I discussed our disappointments, which were multiplying. For two days, our hostess had been serving us tomato salads garnished with feta cheese, but also so much onion that the smell could kill a mosquito, if it dared to approach. Why was she hesitant to listen to our suggestions concerning the menu? Since the first day, I had to show Valerie how to make coffee; you can guess that she surely wasn't hired for her culinary expertise! And, I refrained from mentioning her less-than-courteous attitude. Having seen our hostess' lack of organization, we'd taken the initiative to complete the morning tasks in order to gain some time.

In addition, our departures were still later than planned. Even though Captain John agreed to raise anchor earlier (around 8 or 8:30 a.m.) in order to avoid sailing during the hottest times of the day, he struggled, like the younger passengers, to get out of bed before 9. The maneuvering of the equipment was tiresome and often seemed endless.

Sylvie and I made the same judgment about our situation: There was a considerable gap between what was promised to us – a luxurious, all-inclusive cruise with traditional Greek meals – and what we were actually getting. In other words, we felt cheated.

There's a serious problem, I told myself, and our easygoing captain failed to tackle it. Was this denial of the situation or was he trivializing our needs? Whatever the reason, John's reaction was not a good sign. The disregard for the rules that he established only elevated my level of dissatisfaction. I was glad that Sylvie had the same perception as I did, because it legitimized my need to feel respected. And I felt less alone knowing that we were two (even three) people disappointed in the way the voyage had unfolded.

Later in the afternoon, I noticed that our discussion inspired Sylvie to take action, with accusations against Valerie, who then felt judged in terms of her competence. The two found themselves in a relationship dynamic that was far from constructive. I avoided adding fuel to the fire.

Valerie seemed to be ignoring her role in the emerging conflict. She blamed it on Sylvie's malicious comments and confided in Marie, who offered to help with her tasks and tried to reassure her about the harsh comments that were made. And so, Marie took the initiative to assist Valerie in order to avoid finding herself in an uncomfortable situation. The two supported each other unconditionally, which distanced them from the rest of the crew.

A volatile situation was forming. Given my knowledge of group dynamics, I felt it was my obligation to share my observations with the captain. I very much wanted to avoid an explosion of this conflict. I remained attentive, ready to seize the first available moment I'd have alone with John. Unfortunately, the opportunity for a private moment on a sailboat is rare. And, once evening came, I was too exhausted to start this type of discussion.

Two new crew members arrive

Stephane and Maxime joined us that evening. Two other young people now shared the limited space on board. Would the dissatisfying experiences worsen now? It's a legitimate question. Since the beginning of the cruise, the needs of the two sub-groups had been constantly clashing. The young men's arrival caused an awkward moment for those already on board. However, Stephane's arrival had a positive effect: He had the ability to bond with the entire team. Would he be the one to merge the sub-groups that had formed on the sailboat?

Exercise

List the situations in the sailing story that contributed to the formation of factions within the crew.

_____

_____

_____

If you had been the captain, what would you have done to prevent the cliques from forming?

_____

_____

_____

If you had been a crew member, what would you have done to support the cohesion of the entire group?

_____

_____

_____

Definition of the Faction-Forming Stage

At this point, there is collusion between certain teammates where their bond has formed because of mutual dissatisfaction and hardship.

The formation of clans is inevitable when teammates tolerate their frustrations or have difficulties connecting. It's human nature to try to confirm our perceptions or the sensibility of our expectation by discussing them with one, or a few, colleagues. It's natural to solicit our colleagues to help determine the legitimacy of our needs, especially if they were previously disregarded.

The recognition that our needs are legitimate brings a brief moment of comfort. However, trying to gain support from different colleagues carries the risk that we might contaminate our environment with our judgments, complaints and recriminations. This kind of behavior isn't efficient, especially in trying to improve the situation. If it persists, it leads directly to victimization.

We now better understand why this way of regulating conflicts isn't advocated. Merely exposing your frustrations to someone isn't the mistake. But, if the behavior continues consistently, I can guarantee that the original situation will worsen and that the conflict will extend to every person who was confided in or provided support. The source of dissatisfaction for an individual can quickly become one for several people who share the same values. While the uneasiness spreads, those involved (the clans) lose track of the fact that their attitudes and reactions led them to an impasse and heated, unproductive confrontation.

Clans can form as a result of shared perceptions stemming from misconstrued facts. They exist to relentlessly defend unmet needs. Searching for satisfaction and armed with motives that are more or less constructive, they engage in a stubborn contest, fueled by their contradictory positions.

Circumstances contributing to the formation of factions

1. *The merger of distinct entities without making an effort to unify new colleagues.* A communication activity that brings people together and encourages dialogue can break the ice and open the borders that separate employees coming from different departments.

2. *The delay in trying to integrate the organizational cultures and human resources management policies in the wake of these mergers.* It's impossible to change a company's culture in one day. But, when it comes to people, why delay for months before intervening?

3. *The difficulty in creating a sense of belonging in groups with different needs and realities or groups established in different regions.* Yes, I know, it's not always possible to incorporate every need or desirable to do so at any cost. At the very least, a common goal must be shared.

4. *Opposite values in relation to getting things done.* This increases the chance of confrontations between clans. Adopting a

proven technique based on exemplary results is better than imposing a less-effective course of action simply because it's supported by the faction with the most members.

5. *The absence of regular team meetings.* When a manager confides that he doesn't hold team meetings, I wonder about the team's work climate and its efficiency. In this context, it's not uncommon to find certain employees rallying around common goals and ignoring the needs of other team members.

6. *A division of labor based on pairing up the same people.* Without being aware, we can contribute to the formation of cliques, even though it's unintentional. Constantly collaborating with a select few can alienate the others.

7. *A "divide-and-conquer" management style.* Is it necessary to discuss this obsolete paradigm? If your team members are able to tolerate and help one another in this type of context, it's likely that the situation will eventually turn itself against you. You'll have the impression that you created antagonistic clans: the employees against the boss.

The formation of factions aboard the Lilly

Here is how the formation of clans manifested itself aboard the sailboat.

Causes and indicators

- The fact that the hostess role was split between Valerie and Marie: From the beginning, this turned them into an inseparable duo. Their friendship and solidarity before the conflicts manifested also played a role.

- Ghislaine and Sylvie's union, assisted by the buildup of their dissatisfaction. The two expressed their expectations but were unable to immediately accomplish any improvement.

- Captain John's lack of intervention when it came to the divergent needs of the two subgroups.

- The crew's disregard for the rules of conduct and the captain's complacency on the matter.

- The two late arrivals, whose addition served to strengthen the younger clan.

My experience on the *Lilly* taught me a lot about the factors that instigate the deteriorating climate during a conflict. I realized that by confiding my feelings and frustrations to Sylvie, I contributed to the worsening of the conflict. My position was no longer neutral; I was caught up in the controversy, regardless of my belief that I could stay neutral by intervening as little as possible. But, in a conflict, it's almost impossible to remain completely neutral. Choosing not to actively participate in the conflict doesn't relieve us of our responsibilities.

We were all part of the conflict, whether directly or indirectly. The crew members who'd observed the deterioration of their work climate without intervening (by convincing themselves that it wasn't their business) passively contributed to the conflict's escalation. **By refraining from intervening in a conflict, or passively tolerating the situation, we inherently support it.**

Some common reactions

- Factions usually adopt the following behaviors:

- Seeking support from other colleagues especially to reinforce their "victim" position.

- Pressuring neutral team members to join a clique.

- Rejecting team members who aren't part of their clan or those who oppose it or choose to remain neutral.

- Clashing of different factions, struggling with opposition and an abuse of power. Some common tactics include competition, coercion, intimidation and oppression.

- Adopting a "winner or loser" strategy.

- Increasing complaints against the "opposing clans" relative to the anomalies and irregularities that are usually expected.

Here are some common reactions we often see from the leader who usually adopts the following behaviors:

- Not paying attention to the problem: mistakenly believing that the people will regroup based on their similarities.

- Reinforcing clans by managing the unit or team as if they were distinct groups.

- Interacting with personnel and delegating tasks and projects by taking into account the existence of factions.

- Acquiescing to the clans' demands, reinforcing their position and strengthening their solidarity.

In the following organizational case, try to identify the signs that clans had formed within the team.

Organizational Case No. 3:

The Merger of Three Departments

The reorganization of several departments within a financial enterprise has resulted in friction. Three departments that had been functioning independently are now one branch called Internal Client Support, composed of three sub-groups. Patrick's team is responsible for IT support management. Normand and Celine's teams consist of various analysts in charge of supporting internal client activities. These three teams need to work together to provide the best support services and information to their clients, including providing current data on investments and financial operations.

Normand's team, a rigorously managed group, is the most advanced in terms of its organizational abilities and relevant skills. Celine, who's worked for a mere four months, manages a team that is continually being redefined. Indeed, constantly changing client demands necessitate new roles and mandates. The significant staff turnover and the extensive training required for new employees (which can take more than three months) also put this team in a difficult situation.

Celine asks Normand to lend her one or two professionals from his team to help her meet the client demands she has fallen behind on. It's a short-term solution. But, Normand's team is overwhelmed as members work on developing new management tools in collaboration with Patrick's team. Patrick's team is equally busy trying to migrate information and data onto a new IT platform. The two leaders have very few resources to offer their colleague.

Celine finds it hard to let go of her colleagues' refusal to help. She believes they're collaborating in their decision not to help her and interprets this as a conspiracy against her. She shares her frustration with her assistant and team. Eventually, Celine and her team convince themselves that the other teams are purposely refusing to collaborate with them. The situation worsens. Discussions become defensive arguments as both parties justify their actions as a result of their priorities. According to Celine, Normand's team should have helped her. She speaks to her manager and criticizes the other leaders' irresponsible attitudes.

From his perspective, Normand sees Celine's request as an order to be followed. Constantly feeling as if he has to bail out Celine's team, he refuses to collaborate with her. His opinion: She needs to figure it out.

As for Patrick, he feels as though he's between a rock and a hard place. Sometimes, it's Normand who describes how uncompromising Celine can be, and other times, it is Celine who displays an irresponsible and scornful attitude toward Normand. Because each hopes to gain support by sharing his or her grievances with Patrick, Patrick's team feels obligated to choose a side. When the situation becomes unbearable, Patrick confides in his manager about the incidents involving his counterparts, asking him to intervene.

The manager, who has already noticed the growing tension during meetings, observes that the remarks usually go through him. Celine and Normand only address each other if necessary. Everyone looks forward to the end of the meeting: Some even leave early claiming they have other obligations or important projects to attend to.

Your analysis

What are the indicators that show the presence of clans?

_____

_____

_____

Beyond structure

This department faces many difficulties. In terms of structural organization and function, here are some of the improvements the manager has tried to institute:

- Clarification of internal procedures

- Clarification of the flow of requests

- Establishment of planned, prioritized activities for the entire department

Despite the improvement of the procedures and structures, the relational difficulties persist. The principal sources of dissatisfaction are a result of collaboration and interaction that some feel were inadequate. Even if organizational factors were the original problem, the cause of the controversy has now shifted to the way the clans interact, ways that continue to elevate the conflict.

Indicators

Here are indications of the formation and perpetuation of clans:

- A conflict results from different needs, inaccessibility to resources, and failure to resolve those two problems.

- The impression that no one wants to help Celine and her team.

- A biased interpretation of the leader's gestures and words, and sharing those unfounded feelings with colleagues before verifying that those assumptions are correct.

- The fact that those involved avoid speaking directly with one another and instead confide in others.

- Unproductive meetings and the fact that they end early, which means that issues are not addressed accordingly.

- The fact that the manager facilitates third-party communications between the factions by playing the role of "messenger."

- The sharply contrasted beliefs that leads to unconditional solidarity between members of their respective clans. For example, Celine spoke to her assistant and team members after Normand's first refusal to help. Therefore, Celine's team shared her beliefs that Normand was intentionally refusing to collaborate with them.

- The pressure placed on individuals not yet part of a clan. In our case, this applied to Patrick and his team.

Getting back on the right track

The abolition of clans is a delicate process. The improvements at an organizational level are not sufficient enough to disband these groups. Because the conflict is relational, you must act on a relational level. The support that comes from sharing mutual dissatisfactions, disappointments and frustrations is a powerful reinforcement. To reverse the situation, it's necessary to prove that their current actions are inefficient and demonstrate to the key players that they are wasting energy and gaining mixed results. To act at this stage of the conflict, you need to reestablish the influences acting on all parties involved. This type of intervention requires finesse, tact, and plenty of diligence and objectivity.

At this stage of the conflict, the leader will feel tempted to intervene as a manager. Indeed, the parties involved will expect him to make decisions regarding their dissatisfactions or the inequalities that are perceived or real. But can he objectively resolve all of his team's differences? The answer is no. **Too often, attempting to understand everything that's happening, the manager feels obliged to determine the causes of the problem. This usually results in finding someone (or some people) to blame. Taking this route is usually a big mistake.** He indirectly leads his team into a "winner-loser" resolution. Looking for the guilty party rarely brings about results that satisfy everyone involved. This way of proceeding rarely yields positive results, so it should be avoided at all costs.

Adopting the role of mediator

Which hat should you wear? The one of proficient manager who can maintain control, or one of mediator to facilitate communication? In fact, the latter is better adapted to resolve conflict. By adopting the role of manager, you'll feel obligated to find the best solution. But, by adopting the role of mediator, you'll help guide the parties involved in determining a solution that meets all of their needs. Mediation is by far the most effective procedure when negotiating demands. To successfully mediate a situation, you need time, energy, and experience in facilitating communication. To learn more about mediation, consult the section on this subject found in Chapter 6 (page 155).

Responsibilities of the leader

A leader needs to create an agreeable climate for the team, but leaders and team members alike are responsible for maintaining that environment. If the leader doesn't intervene at this stage, the conflict rapidly progresses to the next step – escalation. It's easy to see the existence of factions within your team and confrontation among them. The leader shouldn't ignore or deny the situation; at the very least, he should remind his team about the rules of conduct within the organization. For example, in the previous case we studied, the leader could have said: "I don't accept that you're bad-mouthing your colleagues behind their backs. On the same note, I don't accept that they refused to help without a proper reason. We are a team and we need to work together to reach our goals."

Reiterating the rules and the values that everyone should respect may not resolve the situation completely, but at least the leader has attempted to prevent disrespectful behaviors from escalating. If improving the structure of operations doesn't diminish the sources of dissatisfaction, its best to consult external help to manage the relational problems of the team. If the team stops perceiving the leader as a neutral party, an impartial expert will be beneficial and help navigate everyone through this impasse.

Another example illustrates the difficulty in intervening once a leader's influence has been contested and the situation has become unbearable. An employee shows up for work each morning in a bad mood and treats his colleagues abruptly. In doing so, he creates a disagreeable and tense work environment. His colleagues, who can't stand him, begin to avoid him. No one, including the managers, dares to confront him or ask for his assistance. After noticing the side effects of the worker's behavior, several indolent colleagues follow suit. Soon, the group is complaining about the lack of teamwork and the poor climate within the team. Some begin to miss work and the quality workers begin to resent their manager for letting the situation reach this point.

Yes! The leader lost his team's trust and members no longer see him as capable of preserving an equitable work environment. In this situation, it's imperative to try to improve the work climate and regain the trust of your best team players with the help of an experienced professional.

Responsibilities of the team members

It's equally the responsibility of the team members to maintain a healthy work climate and strong relationships with their colleagues. Yes, you've read correctly. It's both the rapport and interactions among colleagues that help determine the work climate, and it's the colleagues that have the greatest influence. In the previous example, it would have been desirable for a colleague to take responsibility for his contribution to the poor atmosphere: he could have gently approached his grumpy colleague and explained that his attitude affected everyone. **If you tolerate your team's negative attitude, don't be surprised when the work climate deteriorates.** It's up to each person to honor the fundamental rules of respect, mutual open communication, teamwork, and so on. Stop tolerating the disregard for these crucial rules; after all, your work climate and your satisfaction depends on them.

Tips to prevent the formation of clans

Here's some advice directed to the leader and team members to help prevent the formation of clans and promote team unity.

Advice for the leader

- *Spot the formation of clans and intervene quickly.* Taking prompt action gives you flexibility in applying various methods that can help dissolve clans. For example, the leader can assign new responsibilities to team members belonging to different groups, forcing them to work together.

- *Reiterate and reinforce the rules of conduct and team values.* By emphasizing rules and the respect, you're taking care of the organizational climate. As a leader, you influence your team and your own conduct indicates the group dynamic you want to establish. Maintaining a positive work environment should be a daily concern.

- *Always think in terms of "teams" and "group projects."* It's not always obvious. Meetings among sub-groups can prove particularly effective, but it's important to promote a team vision and the development of common goals. It's up to you to manage your meeting and choose the strategies best-suited to your situation.

- *Take on the role of mediator.* If you sense a strained rapport between two people, intervene as soon as possible to prevent the formation of clans. A team leader told me: "When I feel that discord exists between two members of my team, I intervene immediately. I invite them to speak in front of me, in my office, and we find solutions. I sense a lot less tension within my team and my role as a leader is much easier to bear. It works!"

- *Intervene between the "hard-core" instigators.* They are those who, without discernment, impress their own frustrations and judgments onto their peers. They are at the source of the formation of clans and, consciously or subconsciously, share the same intention: damaging the other factions. You should arrange private meetings with each individual. But, you need to ensure that the rest of the team will not come to their defense. This type of intervention has a better success rate if it's conducted early in the faction-forming stage. If the factions are already established, the intervention may produce adverse effects; it can fuel the opposition and strengthen the antagonistic position of the clans.

Advice for the team

- *Remain steadfast about the work climate you want.* As previously mentioned, it's the people who determine the quality of their work environment. Don't let it deteriorate.

- *Point out the existence of clans and the discomfort you feel.* In the previous case, Patrick shared that he was uncomfortable giving in to the pressures that the clans placed on his team. It was a good call. Let's say that someone notices that her or his team is working less efficiently (because of the presence of clans) and gains the supervisor's support in this matter. Together, the two can direct the group in question toward a solution that will eliminate the aggravations. Now, this is a constructive approach.

An example of resolution: the dissolution of clans and successful team merging

Going through the stages of resolution by intervening can yield significant results. You can decide for yourself by reading the following examples.

Step 1: *Diagnosis of the climate by the leaders responsible.*

The diagnosis helped determine the list of improvements that were important to the department.

Step 2: *Analysis and convergence of needs and expectations.*

The analysis and convergence of needs brought out the common expectations of all three departments. The reformulation of expectations and objectives to be attained for the team looked like this:

- Stay aware of roles and responsibilities and follow a team-oriented game plan.

- Speak honestly without being defensive.

- Develop trust within the teams and improve the quality of interactions.

- Define the modes of communication and collaboration that best allow team members to work in harmony toward their goals.

- Create a plan of action – vision, objectives, predicted outcomes – and a common plan that reflects the management's priorities.

Step 3: *Individual meetings with Celine and Normand.*

In individual meetings, the antagonists were able to express their expectations and it was easier to progress to a dialogue.

- Normand and Celine were able to escape the rut they were trapped in. The two spoke about their respective positions and perspectives. Normand was able to express his irritation toward Celine's "authoritative and abrupt" way of making demands. On her part, Celine told Normand that she had expected only temporary assistance, while he had believed it would be long-term. Finally, Celine confessed her beliefs that Normand treated her coldly after gaining his position. Resolving the conflicts between Celine and Normand resulted in the dissolution of the factions that had formed.

Step 4: *Presentation of the manager's expectations of his team.*

The goal of this stage is to develop a common reality for the teams in order to better resolve problems.

Step 5: *Two days devoted to the resolution of relational difficulties within the team and the clarification of expectations concerning the leader.*

The team members worked diligently and produced powerful results.

- The other members confessed that the conflict between their teams and Celine and Normand had made them uncomfortable.

- A common agenda was established. A consensus of group priorities diminished the possibility of friction between team members and significantly reduced the pressure.

- The team created an important rule: not to let interpersonal conflicts between team members worsen. They recognized that maintaining an agreeable work climate takes daily effort.

Step 6: *Post-resolution, supporting the managers in maintaining the work climate.*

Three months later, the following are a testament to the team's shared responsibility in maintaining the work climate.

- The team coasted as a result of its efforts, and has been dedicated to its primary mission – supporting the managers by providing the best service.

- The manager regained control of his team and noted the favorable climate that prevailed.

Resolution tools adapted for this stage

If you're asking yourself what you can particularly do to prevent the formation of factions, here are some suggestions.

- *Diagnose the organizational climate.* A diagnosis will help you determine which factors influence the work climate and formulate directions that you can take to help resolve problems.

- *Organize activities to improve communication and the overall work climate.* Any activity that aims to define rules, policies, roles, responsibilities, preserve a healthy work environment, clarify the leader's expectations, and overall address the needs of an unsettled team meets this criterion.

- *Provide the leader with resources to help him develop his knowledge on managing and preserving a healthy work environment.* Some managers simply lack the ability to handle such a climate. A team meeting is a great opportunity to show support in helping your manager and his team attain their goals.

- *Mediate between people.* Early mediation can prevent or halt the formation of clans before the situation becomes uncontrollable.

- *Intervene within the team.* This is necessary when clans have existed for a while and the leadership has been questioned and its credibility tainted.

Summary

Stage 3: The Formation of Factions

Collusion between certain team members as a result of shared dissatisfaction, mutual grievances and hardship.

	Symptoms/Indicators Present	Tips and Techniques to Prevent The Formation of Clans	Signs of Improvement
Energy Type	• Residual energy		• Cohesive energy
Climate	• False harmony or agreement; distrust	• Diagnosis of organizational climate	• Improvement in degree of trust
Communication	• Clans confront one another overly	• Activities to improve communication and work climate; rules of conduct, roles and responsibilities, expectations according the leader, etc.	• More communication among team members who didn't speak beforehand
Interpersonal Relationships	• Any ideas suggested by the opposing clans are rejected.	• Mediation: intervening when inappropriate behaviors and attitudes surface or there is conflict between two people	• A gradual dissolution of clans: • Team members begin to distance themselves from their former clans and focus on their individual needs
Work Teams	• Members within the same clan support one another, but there is little interaction with other clans	• Reassigning tasks, assigning responsibilities and projects so as to promote communication between clans; intervening within a team; dissolving clans by going after the hard-core instigators	• Dissolution of clans: It's possible to return to a normal, functional unit without clans
Attitudes	• A strong belief that opposing clans have malicious intentions	• Create a committee, which consists of members from both clans, to improve work climate	• Willingness to approach other team members and share resources
Needs	• Recognition of needs because of the clan's support	• Guidance from a manager specializing in the work climate	

Formation of Clans ← → Cohesion

Frequent Reactions

From the Team Members	From the Leader
Seeking the approval or confirmation of team members' feeling the same deceptions, disillusions and dissatisfactions	Misunderstanding the phenomenon behind the formation of clans; falsely believing that team members are truly bonding
Pressuring neutral team members	Reinforcing clans (voluntarily or involuntarily)
Rejecting team members who don't wish to be part of a clan	Interacting and delegating projects in a way that supports the clans
Causing conflict between clans, struggles and opposition extending to even an abuse of power	Favorably responding to the clans' demands, thereby reinforcing them
Adopting a "winner-loser" attitude	
Multiplying grievances	

CHAPTER 4: ESCALATION AND EXPLOSION

THE SAILING STORY

John suggested a swim in the sulfurous waters of Santorini and awakened everyone's enthusiasm. Finally, after four days of cohabitation, everyone shared a positive reaction.

Our brief scheduled stop for lunch went awry. Sylvie found out that Valerie served us the leftovers of a salad from the night before, which had been left out on the counter overnight. Insulted and disgusted, she harshly berated Valerie. A heavy silence settled into the cockpit, where we all were seated. Not knowing what to do, the captain made some excuses and the humiliated hostess disappeared into her cabin.

Once again, Sylvie told the captain her numerous dissatisfactions: the questionable freshness of certain foods, the noncompliance of our demands, the irregular meal and departure times, and the lack of fresh, bottled water. Like any leader at fault, the captain promised to remedy the situation. Sylvie appeared to be relieved and exclaimed, "It's about time!" Do we need to shout to gain respect? I don't like to get there, but I want the services that we paid for!"

A belated clarification of roles

The captain joined Valerie in her cabin and the two started an animated discussion. Valerie was insulted and found it unjust that all the blame was placed on her. She challenged John's position, claiming that he never clearly defined her role and that his directions were contradictory. She added, "And, Sylvie is always angry and always on my back and you let her be and choose not to intervene … ."

A necessary discussion on the current climate

We anchored in a bay where we could all go for a swim. While the others swam, I approached the captain and discussed the difficulties with the climate on board. I had hoped that this discussion would have taken place before the altercation that had just taken place, but John would likely be more inclined to address the issues now.

The captain briefly analyzed the afternoon's quarrel. According to him, it's due to an incompatibility between Sylvie and Valerie. Sylvie had a critical temperament and was quick to criticize Valerie. Valerie, a spoiled child with little work experience, had a hard time accepting Sylvie's comments. John offered this conclusion: "Now that they've spoken their minds, things should go better. I spoke to Valerie; she will put aside her pride and sensitiveness and try not to overreact to Sylvie's comments."

This reaction was typical of a nonchalant leader. I explained that there was more at stake than clashing characters and that the afternoon's incident was a symptom of deeper issues. I added, "You need to assume stronger leadership over managing the climate on board. If not, it will become unbearable." The captain, unfortunately, took a step back. "You'll see," he replied, "time will fix things."

"John, time never fixes things; it can only aggravate them," I replied. "This isn't a team that you have on board, but two clans: the young 'disrespectful' one, and the older 'dissatisfied' one, with the exception of Stephane, who seems to belong to neither group. These cliques don't share any interests and their needs and lifestyles are completely opposed. The climate is so disagreeable that I intend to shorten my vacation by leaving the *Lilly* a week earlier than expected."

John seemed shocked by what I said. Was it possible that he never noticed any of the things I mentioned: the two sub-groups whose opposing needs had made it difficult to reconcile; the lack of clear roles; the unjust situation (unpaid passengers) that hadn't been explained; the recent escalation, showing that no one was willing to put "water in their wine?" All of these incidents that I put into context and showed their interrelation seemed to have escaped his attention.

He also neglected a crucial factor: the lack of real direction. On a boat, there is only one captain and he exercises great influence over his team. His role on board is not to simply give directions to his crew on what needs to be done. A good captain takes necessary decisions, balances the objectives and needs of those on board and creates a respectful and collective climate. By letting the situation run its course, John implicitly endorsed the difficult climate on the *Lilly*.

"Do you know that I've made several cruises with diverse groups and have never faced this kind of situation?" John confided. "I assure you, Ghislaine, this is the first time it's happened." First time or not, I told myself, earlier experiences are not always indicators of future ones. Each team has its own character, dynamic and temperament. I announced to the captain, "In all honesty and straightforwardness, I think we are headed straight for the outbreak of the conflict on board. The escalation has already begun and it will soon follow."

The discussion ended when the other team members returned. John seemed concerned.

An attempt at resolution

By the end of the day, we had cast anchor in a small port southeast of Thira. The captain drove us to a store that rented mopeds and said, "Here, tonight you have free reign." We were all surprised by this improvised plan.

Before slipping away, John announced: "So! Today we encountered some problems on board. With what concerns the food, I spoke to Valerie, and some changes will be made. We will take care to serve you more varied meals and Valerie will ask you your preferences. However, for the meals, we have to consider the foods that are available on the islands."

"OK," we all mumbled in response.

John continued, "As for the morning, per Ghislaine's request, we need to wake up a little earlier and leave before 9 a.m. to stay on our course. Ghislaine will be in charge of waking us up. As for you, Valerie, you need to take care of your errands in the morning make sure you are ready for our departure. For tonight, I want to take a little break and spend some quality time with my nephew. Have a good night, everyone!"

The captain's abrupt and lukewarm tone had the same effect on us as a cold shower. It was as if he had told us, "I've seen enough of you all. I need a break!"

The young crew went in a different direction than the paying passengers. In Guy and Sylvie's company, I realized that I felt pretty well and that four days had already passed in a state of constant tension. On a sailboat, in such a confined space, four days can seem an eternity.

In the morning, the smell of bacon woke us up early. The girls prepared us an American-style breakfast. That night, Maxime took charge of preparing a spaghetti sauce from scratch and served us a delicious dinner. On board the *Lilly*, the storm seemed to have settled. The previous day's incident gave rise to adjustments that reflected everyone's needs. It was not too late! I was delighted to see that my predictions were wrong. Hopefully, our team would find a common rhythm.

Exercise

List all of the situations that contributed to the escalation and altercation between the crew members.

_____

_____

_____

If you were the captain, what would you have done to prevent the conflict from worsening?

_____

_____

_____

If you were a crew member, what would you have done to promote the group's cohesion?

_____

_____

_____

The definition of the Escalation and Explosion Stage

This stage is characterized by open and sometimes abusive confrontation because of the reliance on a win-lose mentality. The escalation occurs when the unmet needs become too numerous and the final straw breaks the camel's back. As in the case of the *Lilly*, it can surface at an unexpected moment. Sometimes, a scene can be caused by a seemingly innocuous event or detail. The people who observe the situation are often shocked and may find the emotional response to be an overreaction.

In any case, escalation is always pervasive among the clans. The fundamental needs are expressed at whatever cost in order to gain support and power. The parties involved will go as far as to use intimidation to defeat their opponents. Reprehensible behaviors might provoke confrontation and the struggle between clans. Some examples of such conduct include trying to offend or humiliate a person in front of others or verbal attacks that belittles someone publicly. In situations where the conflict has lasted for a long time, some insults reach the level of psychological harassment. And, in some cases, those who are the target of aggression file a complaint in order to stop the hostile behaviors toward them.

What drives people to escalation? Frustration and a lack of tools to effectively communicate their needs and expectations. The feeling that others are failing to hear them out. Feeling threatened. An example: Feeling that Clan B is benefitting from an advantageous position, Clan A prepares a defense by never missing the opportunity to bring Clan B down. You've well understood that this stage is a power struggle where there can only be a single winner.

When the process of escalation has begun, the explosion of conflict becomes the only outcome for clans. Locked in a vicious circle, they manifest their hostility by increasingly derogatory remarks and violently hateful words. They think that is the only way to end the attacks against them. But, by asserting themselves more and more, they inevitably lead themselves toward an outburst. It is interesting to note that only outside observers see the inefficiency of this process; the clans involved have lost all objectivity.

Circumstances contributing to the Escalation and Explosion

1. *Unequal distribution of power and resources.* For example, within a team, the same people always benefit from the biggest budget.

2. *The lack of management of the work environment.* If we can manage a conflict, we can also manage the atmosphere within a team. Need I mention that the manager can define rules of conduct conducive to creating the climate he desires?

3. *The lack of real leadership.* Examples: a manager who is absent due to long illness; important decisions that are constantly postponed; a manager at the controls who doesn't make decisions.

4. *Mismanaged mergers in which policymakers did not intervene in the climate.* By letting clans fight or ignoring conflict, you are paving the way for escalation.

5. *Tolerance of disrespectful, even hateful, behaviors.* This provokes the intensification of hostile and aggressive conduct. The new laws against psychological harassment in the workplace are designed to avoid such situations, as they support those who want to work in a violence-free environment.

6. *An accumulation of unfair situations that managers endure without opening dialogues on the matter.* By closing your eyes to the abuse of your employees (e.g., an abuse of work hours or vacation), you encourage the outbreak of conflict.

Escalation aboard the Lilly

Here is how the escalation manifested itself on the sailboat.

Causes and Indicators

- A repeated expression of unmet needs and an absence of timely corrective actions.

- A noncompliance of basic needs and agreements, which led to an accumulation of frustration.

- An ambiguity of roles. For example, Valerie was not fulfilling her duties, and the captain left the crew to deal with their own operational difficulties.

- Valerie's incompetence and her stubbornness, which caused her to ignore the other passengers' suggestions.

- An unjust situation (such as free transport of certain passengers) that was not explained.

- The fact that a team member (Ghislaine) intended to leave the group.

- The energy and time lost discussing the same controversial subjects, such as the team's needs.

- The demands made in an aggressive way by Sylvie. The language and tone used should have served as a warning for the captain.

- An absence of leadership: John completely neglected the quality of the relationships and climate on board his boat. He confined himself to the role of navigator.

- The captain's incorrect analysis of the climate that prevailed on board: According to John, the tension was due to a character incompatibility between Sylvie and Valerie.

The explosion aboard the Lilly

All the circumstances listed here contributed to the outburst: Sylvie berated Valerie in front of the others because she was unable to endure the injustice, discomfort and poor service – all things she attributed to the steward. The intensity of her reaction should have caused any leader to react. Justified or not, her warning said, "I've had enough, this needs to stop!"

During an ongoing conflict, the needs and challenges are not necessarily clearly verbalized by the parties involved. **The escalation is often only the tip of the iceberg.**

Some frequent reactions

How do people react when involved in a conflict? It depends on their temperament. For example, combative people can adopt defensive behaviors and boldly try to defend their position and defeat the opposing party. On the other hand, more unobtrusive people will just look to survive this troubling period.

Here are some reactions that are often observed when a conflict progresses to this stage:

- *Temporarily withdrawing (from the team).* People who, like Guy, have a very low level of tolerance for negative emotions have the tendency to avoid people or situations that provoke such events.

- *Escaping.* It often happens that the best talent will seek more pleasant and satisfying work environments. Because they possess skills that are sought after, they see more benefit in leaving than staying.

- *Winning through struggles: breaking the opposing party.* Because frustration has exceeded the acceptable threshold and the climate is unhealthy, the loss or abandonment of convictions comes at a great psychological loss. The losing person or clan must face the other party to restore image and credibility.

- *Judging the leadership.* The credibility of the leadership is lost when the team members begin to note the absence of appropriate decisions and interventions regarding conflicting relationships. The team no longer counts on the manager's leadership.

- *Complaining.* The objections have to do with the attitudes among colleagues and may lead to filing complaints of psychological harassment.

- *Fighting.* In extreme cases, it's a real battlefield. Yes, there are people who can't live without conflict and they will do anything possible to maintain a hostile climate. And, once they succeed, it drives them to engage in a power struggle. Some people also define themselves by their ability to oppress others and forget that they have the ability to choose their battles. I agree, it's difficult to change those attitudes. To do so requires a profound knowledge of the types of dominant personalities involved. The only way to effectively intervene is to make them aware of their suffering. As odd as this seems, these are suffering people who are engaged in "survival mode." In order to escape their own sufferings, they try to make others suffer.

When I intervened in a crisis situation, I observed the following reactions among managers.

- *Relying on "magical thinking."* Recognizing that the work environment was unhealthy, but feeling helpless in the matter, the managers maintained hope that time would sort things out.

- *Panicking.* The management is struck with a sense of paralysis before the events take an unexpected turn. The outburst of conflict becomes a rude awakening. Panicked, the leadership quickly seeks out the help of the human resources department.

- *Asking for help.* The managers request assistance or support from the human resources department or other competent advisors. Some have felt the first tremors before the earthquake. Whew! They narrowly avoided being crushed. Others never saw it coming. For example, an unexpected incident can provoke a thunderous altercation between two people, without the former stage happening.

Too often, the managers do not recognize the severity of the situation at this stage. Although the damage has already been done, it's not too late to act. However, you need to support the psychological and financial costs associated with such a conflict and arrange for sufficient effort in order to regain everyone's confidence.

Now, from the following organizational situation, try to identify the indications that predict an escalating conflict and its imminent explosion.

Organizational Case No. 4

The Explosion Within a Team of Secretaries

A conflict has been building for two years within a team of four secretaries. Three of them, Louise, Diane and Michelle, have worked together for seven years. The fourth, Maggie, works a temporary position but has been a regular replacement for the last year.

Between Louise and Diane, it's war. For more than two years the two women haven't spoken and have avoided each other. No longer able to stand the conflict, Louise has been on sick leave for eight months. A dispute from five years ago has had unfortunate consequences. Louise, no longer willing to come to Diane's aid on a professional or personal level, has taken her distance. Diane, offended by her friend and colleague's reaction, has begun to belittle her. Through their disputes, they have each sought support from their other colleagues. Michelle supports Diane and Maggie supports Louise or her replacement when Louise is on a sick leave. There are now two cliques. As they are stuck in the same small office and often lack privacy, the secretaries spy on each other quite often.

The two clans are fueling the conflict by filing complaints with their union about the behavior and attitudes of the others. Michelle complains of the strong smell of Diane's perfume, and she often warns the manager of Maggie's tardiness. Everything is subject to controversy: the location of a plant, the temperature of the office, some people's tardiness and other's holidays. Envy and jealousy are not lacking. The manager has tried to solve the problem, suggesting different ways to deal with the limited space and reinforcing regular rules of conduct, but everything has failed.

The manager now feels like a hostage of the two clans. If he agrees to the demands of one secretary, he turns his back on the others. Maggie, angered that her claims were not satisfied, files a complaint to her union. This time, her manager is shocked: Maggie is accusing Diane of psychological harassment.

The leader organizes a meeting between the five in order to halt the escalation and to end these issues once and for all. Once the secretaries are in front of one another, the dispute erupts. Disrespectful words flow from all sides. The manager tries to stop this hateful exchange. Too late, the spell has been cast. The meeting is a failure.

Everyone leaves frustrated. They resent the manager for having dragged them into a pointless discussion. In the following days, the climate is so tense in the office that employees or colleagues from other departments avoid coming in that office. The manager, alarmed by the decline in the situation he caused, feels paralyzed. A human resources professional recommends that he consult an external source to resolve the conflict.

Your analysis

What do you think are the indicators that reflect the escalation that led to the breakup?

_____

_____

_____

The quest for power

Some people are bad players, whereas others are not. In a conflict, the former will have a hard time letting go. Very often, during the escalation, the reason for the fight is no longer important. What's important is not letting the other party win, not losing face. This period is by far the least productive. Each party is mobilizing its energy and efforts to attack the others while defending and protecting him or herself. Do not be surprised if you then see a considerable production decrease.

The conflict can also become totally irrational. For example, Diane was convinced that Maggie had complained against her because she wanted to "break her." In fact, Maggie wanted to be protected against her colleague's outrageous negativity. We frequently attribute malevolent intentions to our adversaries and it becomes difficult to dispel such an impression. An open dialogue can therefore be useful to encourage them to clarify their intentions and express their needs, and so begin to reverse the unhealthy process that has started.

The responsibilities of the leader

At this stage, the leader feels incapable of managing the work environment. As his credibility is tainted, he needs to act cautiously and clearly state his intentions. Ideally, in the process of conflict resolution, he should be accompanied by an objective outside expert.

The idea of holding a meeting with his team was not bad. However, the fact that he didn't clearly announce his intentions, reasons for the meeting, or the way it would proceed provoked a defensive reaction in his team. Because they weren't prepared for the meeting, the secretaries felt trapped and reacted accordingly. If you force opponents to face one another, each will want to land the first strike in order to have the best chance for escape. This is exactly the way most people react when they feel threatened by a conflicting relationship.

The meeting could have been organized in such a way to prepare the parties to formulate their needs and expectations in a constructive manner. A neutral party (other than the manager, obviously) could have mediated and helped bring the parties to resolve their conflict, all while enforcing basic rules, such as forbidding inappropriate language and personal attacks. A mediator would have supervised the discussion and helped the parties focus on a single goal. The idea is to gain everyone's agreement on a certain point, which will eventually bring together their opinions on more contentious issues.

An example: During the resolution of a team conflict, the manager noted that two employees who were cousins would constantly belittle each other in front of their colleagues. He did not want them to contaminate the work atmosphere, and asked me how to react. He was worried, because a squabble between the two cousins had disrupted the production line the day before. Agreeing that he was not impartial, we decided to meet the two cousins together and force them to examine the behaviors that were disturbing the entire team. The manager would observe my intervention and take part when he felt his role as manager was relevant. The rules of engagement were given at the beginning: no profanity, no personal attacks, only respectful, well-formulated thoughts in the first person would be entertained. Yet, three minutes later, the discussion unraveled. After giving them three warnings, I had to stand up to silence the two rivals. The manager and I took advantage of that little episode to make them aware of their reactions and the consequences of those reactions.

Observing a mediation is a wise way to learn at this stage. Those learning experiences will eventually be useful for preventative management of an emerging conflict between two people. Hearing rivals express themselves without intervening allows you to first experience a reaction to other's negative emotions and can help in mastering control over conflicting situation. I often ask managers what they find the most difficult in such a circumstance. All, without exception, have told me that it is staying impartial and not reacting personally to the emotions that are being expressed. It's difficult to silence your own sympathies for or against someone or avoid the trap of trying to determine who is right or wrong. In the case I just described, my client made me a central part of his learning process. "I never thought I could reconcile these two employees." One of the cousins, in fact, had started to cry. Seizing the opportunity, I was able to calm her emotions as she transitioned from anger to sadness, from sadness to disappointment, and from that to expressing her needs, all in less than 90 minutes.

The responsibilities of the team

At this stage, we can add fuel to the fire by demanding that the team act in a reasonable manner, thereby provoking a guilty reaction. However, most of the time, the parties implicated in a conflict already feel guilty, and by reinforcing that, we do not promote a resolution. Yes, the team members are responsible for their words, conducts and actions. We need to educate them of the consequences of their actions: If they push their limits, they must face the sanctions of their managers or employer.

Sometimes, people are aware of the inefficiency of their actions. They feel that their energy is spent in an unproductive way and that their suffering is only increasing, so they seek help. It is very important to respond to these requests as quickly as possible. Very few people are trained in conflict resolution. Most of our knowledge comes from life experience. While some people may be familiar with constructive approaches such as collaboration or searching for a compromise, others only know one inflexible strategy: competition.

Each person is responsible for his or her actions. If a conflict occurs, we can, in an attempt to resolve it, head in some particularly interesting directions: participating in relevant workshops; seeking more knowledge on the matter by reading or asking colleagues how they would react in a similar situation. To learn more about attitudes that promote conflict resolution, you can purchase a booklet called *The Thomas-Kilmann Conflict Mode Instrument*.[3] This tool doesn't guarantee a conflict's outcome, but does offer insight on the efficiency of modes of resolution based on the correlation between methods adopted and their context.

Tips to stop the escalation and prevent the outbreak of a conflict

Here are some tips aimed at the leader and the team to put an end to the escalation of a conflict and help resolve one that has already erupted.

Advice for the leader

- *Demand a "time-out."* If you feel that the escalation has increased and that the outbreak is imminent, announce that you are going to appeal to a conflict-resolution specialist in order to establish a better work climate. After all, even if your leadership is partially challenged, your concern with the work environment will earn you support.

- *Develop a code of conduct in collaboration with your teammates.* It will indicate which behaviors are acceptable and put a stop to those that are not. You can use this method if the conflict has evolved rapidly and recently. But, you will need to constantly monitor any signs of improvement. If it worsens, you'll need to react promptly and accordingly.

- *Take inventory of your teammates' expectations toward you.* Inform yourself of the needs and expectations that individuals feel in regards to your leadership. You'll be surprised to realize the degree of disempowerment felt about their work environment. If this is what characterizes your situation, you should consult with an expert.

- *Don't hesitate to consult a competent resource.* Since this is a crucial step, I recommend an external source to help you diagnose the situation, which must be done with discipline and objectivity. If you seek out support during the resolution, you'll familiarize yourself with the process without having to bear the entire responsibility of the intervention. After an experience like that, you'll be better equipped to prevent potential conflicts in the future.

Advice for the team

- *Alert your team leader.* It's true that, on the *Lilly*, I wasn't successful in warning the captain early enough about the climate that had been established on board. However, by addressing the subject, we can temporarily escape the grips of the conflict, as we are not suffering idly. Asserting your needs in a constructive manner is certainly a positive initiative that will attract the attention of your manager.

- *Don't hesitate to ask for help.* If you feel that the situation has become unhealthy, you need to make every effort possible to seek help. Contact your human resources department or other organizations and services if your manager refuses to listen. Your intention should be to mobilize resources in order to resolve the conflict.

- *Adopt a regressive position.* I know that this attitude doesn't necessarily lead straight to the resolution, but it can help you show a little more objectivity and place a finger on the emotions you're experiencing. By discovering them, you can concentrate once again on your needs and clarifying your expectations.

An example of resolution: the conflict between the secretaries

If we were able to solve the conflict between the secretaries, it's certainly because they were open. Yet, they experienced a failure in terms of reconciliation and were fearful of meeting again. I had to work very hard to inspire the hope they needed in one another to attempt a second resolution.

The findings were unanimous: The four were very wary of one another, had little faith in their managers, and didn't believe it was possible to resolve their disputes.

I gained some ground by getting them to discuss something other than their conflict. After the diagnosis, I was hopeful that their problem could be resolved, but nonetheless, I had to regain their confidence and reduce their fears of another outburst. I suggested they attend a workshop on understanding individual differences using the Myers-Briggs Type Indicator. My intention, clearly stated, was to demonstrate that they had some similarities and a bond. No one believed me. Amused by the challenge that I threw at them, the secretaries agreed to partake in the exercise and succeeded. In fact, they sat together in front of their manager for three hours without a single moment of hostility. The first degree of trust was achieved. The concept of interacting without referencing their differences was a new idea for them.

After creating the conditions conducive to constructive dialogue, I had the colleagues partake in a mutual feedback exercise, which had to be done twice. The first meeting was devoted to the resistance among these women. I listened to them and showed them the impasse they found themselves in while reminding them of their personal responsibility for the harmony of the professional relationships. The feedback exercise produced retroactive results. Diane and Louise were able to talk about their disputes, some dating to five years ago. Both confessed to their colleagues that they'd been fighting for all that time due to a simple misunderstanding. The discussion ended with the unanimous adoption of rules conducive to healthy relationships and climate.

Resolution tools adapted to this stage

If you're asking yourself what you can particularly do to cease the escalation and avoid the explosion of conflict, here are some suggestions.

- *Use relevant resources and develop steps appropriate to the specific situation.* Recognizing the presence of a conflict is the first step in resolving it.

- *Do an organizational diagnosis.* This allows you to determine which factors influence your work climate and find paths leading to positive changes and resolution.

- *Intervene with the team.* Because the conflict has spread to the whole team, the curative approach to conflict is unavoidable at this stage.

- *Hold disciplinary meetings.* Yes, it will be necessary to intervene with people who persist with inappropriate or harassing behavior.

- *Support the manager.* Strong support is needed during this period when the manager, who has lost his credibility, is neither neutral nor fully capable of leading his team. He needs reassurance with respect to his actions and decisions.

The tools above can be applied equally with the tools offered in the following paragraph. After all, conflict is complex and may often necessitate multiple levels of intervention.

- *Make the parties involved understand that their method of problem-solving is unproductive.* By intervening quickly and showing them the ineffectiveness of the winner-loser approach, we can help them discover constructive pathways toward a resolution.

- *Mediation.* When the team conflict is resolved but relational differences persist between two people, mediation can serve as a useful component. But, if you intervene only by mediating at this stage, you risk further aggravating the situation.

Summary

Stage 4: Escalation and Explosion

Overt confrontation, accompanied by hurtful and abusive behavior based on a winner-loser attitude

	Symptoms/Indicators Present	Tools and Techniques to Stop the Escalation and Prevent the Explosion	Indicators of Improvement
Type of Energy	• Unhealthy confrontational energy (rivalry)	—	• Collaborative energy (bonding of parties)
Climate	• Inefficient climate	• Consult experts in conflict resolution and mediation. Consult with trade unions and obtain their cooperation	• Healthier, open climate
Communication	• Presence, between others, of these symptoms: verbal aggression, organizational climate, intimidation tactics	• Explain each step of the resolution process and specify each person's role	• Objections made relate to the disputes rather than individuals • Adoption of common courtesies: respect, listening, honest communication
Interpersonal Relations	• Waste of time, energy, and financial resources caused by the declining relationships	• Diagnose the situation by meeting with all persons involved	• Decrease or stop in reprehensible behavior such as denunciation and aggression
Work Teams	• Inefficiency of the work team because of: increased professional afflictions, requests for leaves of absence, and loss of the best talent	• Encourage the participation of the people involved in the resolution	• Most of the people are invested in resolving the conflict
Attitudes	• Denouncing the conflict, which becomes public: the conflict comes out of the closet!	• Set a code describing acceptable behaviors and halting abusive conduct	• Willingness of the parties to put an end to the "war zone" and a commitment: a more constructive approach
Needs	• Affirming their existence	• Hold disciplinary meetings to cease inappropriate and offensive conduct	• The negotiation of a satisfactory agreement for both parties is considered necessary to resolve the conflict

Escalation and Explosion ←→ Conflict Resolution

Frequent Reactions

From the Team	From the Leader
Temporarily withdrawing	Relying on "magical thinking," feeling powerless
Leaves of absence, quitting	Panicking. After initial paralysis, a brutal awakening when facing escalating events
Winning a confrontation by putting down the opposing party	Seeking out help from human resources professionals or external consultants
Judging the manager	
Complaining: an accumulation of grievances	
Fighting, wanting to win at all costs, which can manifest into verbal or physical aggression and psychological harassment	

CHAPTER 5: ESTRANGEMENT

THE SAILING STORY

The morning of Day 6, I had to threaten the captain to get him out of bed. After three attempts to wake him up, I took a drastic measure and relieved myself of my responsibilities. I brandished a bucket of water and warned him that I was ready to pour it on him if he didn't get up on the spot. He leapt out of bed in a single movement. The departure, scheduled for 8 a.m., didn't take place until 9:15.

Arriving at the port, we planned our evening meal. I offered to help Valerie cook one of my own recipes. Before leaving to stroll around the island with Sylvie and Guy, I left our steward with the list of ingredients to buy. We agreed to reunite at 8:30 p.m. on the boat.

A surprise awaited us on our return. Valerie, Marie and Maxime were playing cards. There was no indication that any errands had been run or that they were waiting to prepare a meal. This time, Guy took the initiative to ask Valerie, "Did you find what we need for our supper?"

Valerie responded nonchalantly, "No. I thought John was going to be running the errands."

Guy, reddening by the minute, grumbled, "And where is the captain?"

"He's taking a nap."

"What have you planned for dinner?"

"Nothing. We're waiting for him to wake up."

With that, Guy took his bag, guided Sylvie to the dock, and exploded with anger, "I have never seen such organization. What a lack of respect and know-how! We had an agreement: Ghislaine offered her help to prepare dinner with you, and you aren't even bothered enough to run the errands. I've had enough of your lack of organization. I took measures before I left…and I plan to enforce the terms of the agreement of the contract and get compensated for the poor quality of services offered. We paid for a holiday that included all the services, I remind you." Because he'd barely said a word until now, his reaction surprised us all.

I ran to join the couple on the dock and tried to calm Guy down. My stomach was in knots, but I much preferred to eat in a restaurant than stay on board. We found ourselves near a tavern; Sylvie and Guy considered their options on how to get out of this impasse. As for me, I considered abandoning this excursion by Day 7 as I couldn't take it anymore. We were still discussing this when John, who found us, asked if he could join us. We agreed.

The debate started. Guy demanded respect; if not … up against a wall, John heard our grievances (for once) and apologized several times. Sylvie insisted that the climate had been unbearable since the very first day. She added, "I can't understand the presence of the young people on board. They don't respect their commitments, pollute the atmosphere – in all senses of the word, as they smoke constantly – and haven't even paid for their trip! We constantly have to compromise when we are the paying passengers!"

John claimed that we simply misunderstood who was responsible for tonight's errands. Sylvie reminded him that this wasn't the first time he claimed it was a mere misunderstanding, and that our patience had limits. She added, "We constantly need to put pressure on someone in order to ensure that our agreements are respected. Look how Ghislaine had to work this morning to drag you out of bed. This is supposed to be a vacation, but what happens aboard the *Lilly* is not relaxing. Late departures, disorganized meals, sleepless nights because of the chatter on the deck ... ."

"I know, you've already told me this," John responded. "What more can I do? I have already warned my crew." After these words, I intervened. I had serious doubts about the captain's ability and willingness to improve the situation. Since our departure from Santorini, I kept hoping that the climate and organization would improve. Now I no longer believed it, so I informed John of my decision. "Tomorrow will be the seventh day of the trip. I'm leaving at the next stop and I want you to reimburse me for the second half of the trip." John dejectedly acquiesced to my demands. He returned to Sylvie: "What do you suggest I do about Valerie? She is young and has no work experience. I'm sorry. I didn't think it would turn out so badly."

Guy told him, "Well, I don't think we should compromise our holiday because of your bad decision ... after all, we paid for a luxury cruise and we still want to benefit from our vacation." Sylvie added that she believed the only solution was to get rid of all the young crew members. "Because we are completely incompatible, you have no choice but to split up the group. Either you keep the young crew or you keep us. And Ghislaine stays with us."

Unsettled, John asked, "But who will make the meals from now on? I can't respect the stipulations of your contract without Valerie." Sylvie answered, "In any case, she doesn't know how to cook, and I must add that until now, it's Ghislaine and I that have done the morning's errands. Valerie's presence is not indispensable."

"OK. I'll tell her tomorrow that she needs to leave."

"I think you misunderstood us. I'm not just talking about our hostess, but all of the younger crew. They didn't pay their way so I don't see why we should have to share the limited space on board with them."

"You want me to send all four of them off?"

"Yes."

"We need a supplemental team to go back up the coast, as it's a difficult course. Stephane has the skills for this type of navigation."

"OK. He can stay. He isn't the one who caused the most trouble. The other three disembark tomorrow morning. And this agreement is final."

Sylvie then asked: "Ghislaine, will you stay with us under these new circumstances?" I really wanted to experience a voyage where everyone on board got along, where we didn't need to negotiate the rules every day. This perpetual back and forth exhausted me. My objective was to have fun and relax. And, if the atmosphere were to become less tense, it would already be an improvement. I was ready to try a second time.

John sighed: "OK, before returning on the boat, give me 30 minutes to inform Valerie, Marie and Maxime of our agreement. It's not going to be easy. Tomorrow, we'll leave the port without them. We'll be five on board for the rest of the voyage."

During this time, Sylvie and I began planning the organization of life aboard the boat and … the captain's as well.

Day 7: "Spring Cleaning"

After the departure of the three crew members that morning, Sylvie and I started cleaning. We cleaned everything; we got rid of spoiled food in the cooler and made a list of foods to buy. We also discovered reserves of bottled water, hidden in the young women's cabin.

The *Lilly* moved at a speed of eight or ten knots toward the island of Simi. What a relief! The air was light. I could see the satisfaction in my crew members' eyes. Even the captain was more at ease with us. We discovered his sense of humor. We felt happy. Nevertheless, it's sad to have used such drastic measures, dropping three teammates! We know that the best teams have to face their share of difficulties, and our group was unable to overcome them. Ultimately, we had to amputate three members to save five. Wondering what could have been done to avoid the worst, I was overcome by feelings of guilt and failure. Yet, that was not my responsibility. I imagine that Valerie, Marie and Maxime must have felt rejected. It's unfortunate that we had reached that point of no return.

Exercise

List the factors that drove the team to estrangement.

_____

_____

_____

If you had been the captain, what would you have done to avoid this?

_____

_____

_____

If you had been a crewmember, what would you have done to reconcile the team (supposing it was possible at this point)?

_____

_____

_____

Definition of the Estrangement Stage

Breaking up the team. Some players leave of their own volition; others must be shown the way out. Indeed, when individuals no longer contribute to the team in a positive way, we must face the facts. Before you lose your best players, its best to "clean house" and let go of those who no longer want to work constructively within the organization. I know, very few managers are comfortable with the idea of dismissing an employee. Moreover, if he's fired because of his attitude, a case needs to be built against him, which requires both time and energy.

Estrangement occurs when there is no possibility of reconciliation. When teammates or others involved in a conflict abandon any hope of satisfying their needs, they choose to quit the antagonistic environment in search of a better one. For example, if a conflict endures, skilled workers will not hesitate to leave. Sometimes they leave in the previous stage, no longer able to tolerate constant war around them.

Aside from dismissals and dislocations due to voluntary departures, some estrangements do not come from actions: They are the psychological dropouts. How many employees can you count, off the top of your head, who have already checked out of your organization but continue to collect a paycheck? They certainly affect the work environment by draining the motivation of those around them. Eventually, they'll discourage even their most ambitious colleagues. In this case, the manager faces a climate characterized by apathy. He constantly needs to make an effort and invest energy to counter the demobilization and inaction of his employees.

We can also observe a consistently cold climate. This is the case when people who can't quit their jobs – usually for financial reasons – feel forced to work with colleagues with whom they've broken their ties. The consequences of this situation are heavy to bear for all. Forced to deal with the constraints that such a situation imposes, the manager must hesitate to ask certain people to collaborate. He might even need to use strategies that allow them to avoid each other, such as physically distancing them in the office or assigning them to different services. It's both difficult and unpleasant to manage such a situation: It's as if, after a divorce, the couple were determined to live under the same roof. If you are managing several "divorcees" of sorts in your organization, don't be surprised to see a high turnover rate in your staff.

In summary, estrangement can take three forms:

1. A voluntary departure of certain players;

2. The dismissal of others;

3. The severance of ties of cooperation and trust amongst personnel, between personnel and managers, or between personnel and the organization.

Situations contributing to estrangement

1. *Non-resolution of conflict.* If your organization's culture favors the non-resolution of conflict, I encourage you to count the number of people your organization has lost, and those who have lost motivation. The result of this exercise should lead you to question the efficiency of your management style.

2. *Non-credible leadership.* Once more, managers are involved. Managing personnel includes the work environment, any conflicts, and employees who perform poorly or not at all. If you haven't intervened yet, it's you who will be blamed for the departure of the quality players.

3. *A persisting unhealthy work climate.* Sometimes, the organization culture prevails on the goodwill of the individuals. If this group is notorious for having a high staff turnover, its reputation will spread and deter the well-intentioned players.

Estrangement aboard the Lilly

Here is how estrangement manifested itself aboard the sailboat.

Causes and Indicators

- The multiplication of unresolved organizational problems and the unhealthy climate that resulted.

- The feelings of injustice and abuse because of the inexperience and incompetence of the hostess, which led to noncompliance of the expected services.

- The behavior of the hostess, which announced the estrangement: She ignored the passengers and their demands.

- In certain team members, a loss of faith in the willingness and ability of the captain to solve the conflicts.

- A passengers' showing the intention of leaving (in Stage 4).

- The use of power: The paying passengers used their bargaining power to force the captain to choose between the two clans. This strategy always leads to estrangement.

The departure of certain team members didn't automatically lead to the resolution of the conflict. The crew members on board still felt a sense of disillusion and failure. **We got rid of the symptoms but not the captain's underlying organizational problem.**

Frequent reactions

Here are some frequent reactions among the team members:

- *Numerous departures.* If the best players are confident that they can thrive elsewhere, they'll be the first to leave, and others will follow.

- *Various forms of avoidance,* such as: ignoring one person or refusing to work with him or participate in his work. Actions are guided by apathy. This is estrangement in its passive mode.

Here are some frequent reactions of the managers:

- *Delayed reactions, until the very last minute.* By behaving like the *Lilly's* captain, who acted the ostrich since the very beginning, the manager finds himself in a lose-lose situation: His bargaining power and his ability to act positively on the work climate become virtually nothing.

- *Professional exhaustion.* This is not surprising since, at this point, the manager is constantly sailing against the current. The downturn is inevitable.

- *Resignation.* Some captains will leave their sinking ship; not feeling support from upper management, they'll prefer to save their own skin rather than undergo a complete failure. After all, it becomes a matter of survival.

The following case will allow you to observe all the indicators and symptoms of a conflict that has reached its final stage: estrangement. The following exercise is different from those accompanying the previous stages. I invite you to associate with each stage of conflict the indicators or triggering events that you've identified. Doing so will test your understanding of each stage as well as your ability to recognize their symptoms. If a similar situation seems to form in your organization, you'll be able to prevent the conflict or act before it worsens. It's your turn to play now.

Organizational Case No. 5

A Conflict Among Professors

In an academic institution, a department is experiencing a colossal conflict that has lasted for four years. Certain events exacerbated it, such that the estrangement stage has been reached.

The department had experienced significant growth, notably because the school tried to establish new, specialized programs. As a result, the department recruited six new instructors within the last year. The recruitments were made in accordance with the rules. Once the new teachers took office, they forged links with colleagues teaching in the same discipline. Their integration was progressive, except for one case, Julie.

A laborious integration

Julie feels that her colleagues do not act fairly toward her. Indeed, weeks elapse before she gets a desk, computer and other equipment. Julie begins the fall session without settling in properly. She lets her supervisor know of her needs. Despite his promises, another week passes and nothing has changed. She begins to worry.

Then, when she finally gets a workstation, its network connection doesn't work. She lets the IT department know of the problem. Again, there is a delay in responding to her request. When she asks her colleagues whether these delays are normal, she is told that they're rather unusual. Some of her colleagues believe that the supervisor, with the support of other colleagues, is deliberately trying to sabotage her by causing these delays. According to them, this clique is envious of her expertise. Julie can't believe it. She contacts her supervisor and insists that he intervene with the IT department. He tells her that the situation is normal and that, early in the semester, the service is always overwhelmed because of the new faculty's arrival. After two more weeks, the network connection is finally fixed.

The need for new rules of operation

The more players in the game, the clearer the rules need to be. But, some professors in the department, about 20 people, are more or less explicit. The recruitment of new teachers presents an opportunity to clarify or modify these conventions. Thus, certain professors would like a review of the distribution of course loads in relation to budget allocation and grant privileges. But their suggestions are not entertained. An unspoken rule appears to be: "Disturbing the mode of operation that has been in place for many years is not allowed."

As the school year unfolds, the departmental meetings are marked by increasing tension. The head, pressured by some of his colleagues, proposes an amendment of the current course distributions, which others strongly oppose. They cry "favoritism" and the members of the department confront one another, citing current or past situations they deemed unfair. It's the beginning of the escalation stage. The supporters of change face those who choose the status quo. Meetings are now unproductive; the words exchanged become increasingly disrespectful.

Outside of meetings, the newly hired professors (except for Julie) feel as though they're walking on eggshells. They feel pressured to join one of the two forming sub-groups. Some of their colleagues approach them in the hallways, and, condemning the opposing party, ask for their support.

The incident

Months pass without any changes. A triggering event, the professors evaluations, will have a devastating effect on the work climate. Indeed, one of the clans is convinced that an assessment was made unfairly. The person responsible for the cause of unfair assessment had to submit his resignation. The two clans argue in a public arena. There is no respect or consideration. The escalation of the conflict leads to reprehensible behavior: defamation, verbal threats, and intimidation of colleagues trying to remedy the situation.

Senior management has tried to untangle the firmly rooted conflict. Three attempts at reconciliation, supported by an outside administrator, have failed. The rule that characterizes the conflict: triumphing at any cost over the other clan. Engaged in an unhealthy and unproductive struggle, the sub-groups have lost all sense of objectivity. Antagonizing one another has become their purpose, their sole way of defining themselves. In the course of this battle, they've lost four excellent professors who decided to seek employment elsewhere.

Faced with this volatile situation and having failed at intervening, senior management decides to seek out external resources. At that stage, the following symptoms are present:

- A voluntary departure of competent individuals.

- A high occurrence of sick leave.

- Opposition of the two clans.

- A lack of communication and confidence.

- Attempts in blaming the other party.

- Hostile behaviors such as contempt, malicious allusions, intimidation, threats.

- Isolation of certain people.

- Rejection of any new solutions or leaders.

- Attitude characterized by a vicious war: Each party is determined to win at all costs.

Your analysis

Associate the signs or triggering events at each stage of the conflict.

Stage	Indicators or triggering events
Exclusion	
Confrontation	
Formation of Factions	
Escalation and Explosion	
Estrangement	

Responsibilities of the leader

In the case described above, the leader attempted to rectify the situations that he and his colleagues deemed unfair. His bias, as he was the leader of one the clans, affected his approach and certainly his leadership. The members of the other clan saw his behavior only as manipulative and an abuse of power. Any attempts by him were doomed to failure. Because he was a professor and he had just been promoted to a management position, confidence in his leadership had not yet been established. In fact, he was accused of not intervening quickly enough to Julie's issues, trying to change the rules, and having unjustly evaluated a professor, the latter in complicity with a committee.

Although his initial intentions may have been praiseworthy, the way he went about them led to criticism. When a leader fails to impose his authority and can only exert some influence, he should try to gain support from the majority of the team in order to succeed in making changes. His mistake was to consult only colleagues who shared his vision, and seek only their support. Because he acted with obvious bias, his actions weren't well received by the other clan.

It would have been wiser on his part to make his appeal to the hierarchy or to a third party that could have helped him modify the rules of the department. In fact, given the increasing number of employees and new teachers, it was necessary to institute new rules or update the old ones in light of emergent needs.

Responsibilities of the team

The professors equally contributed to tarnishing their work environment. By supporting one or the other clan, they reinforced the opposing dynamic that had formed. Although they requested help from the human resources department, it unfortunately came a little too late. A climate of opposition had already been established.

It's difficult for the new hires to remain completely outside of the game that is being played. In fact, the constant encouragement, as implicit as it may be, from colleagues to join one clan or another are difficult to ignore. I experienced a similar situation in the context of education. Noting the existence of two clans since my recruitment and not wanted to be mixed into the mess, I went straight to the personnel manager and asked for an office outside of the department. I had peace for a year, but I lost a tremendous amount of influence over my colleagues. I had withdrawn from them and so they excluded me. During departmental meetings, they made it clear to me that I was looked upon as an external agent whose remarks were not as credible.

At this stage, interventions between pairs must be handled diplomatically. For example, you can tell one colleague: "The problem you are dealing with is not mine. Have you ever considered expressing your expectations to him or her?" And you must repeat often that sharing his problems with everyone except the source will only worsen the situation.

There is always one person within a team who has a positive influence on all of his colleagues. Aboard the *Lilly*, this was Stephane. His character and ability to interact easily with both sub-groups could have benefitted the team. For example, the captain could have asked this young man to promote a team spirit and bring together the sub-groups. People such as Stephane possess a certain charisma, easily ascertain relational difficulties, and can often resolve them. It costs nothing to consult them, and above all, exploit their skills.

Tips for successful reconciliation

No attempt to resolve the issues internally can succeed at this time. It makes no difference whether the manager works alone or finds support from the human resources department. Because the parties involved no longer believe in reconciliation, communication has been broken for a long time, and the problem has become personal, reconciliation is more likely to succeed if a credible and impartial third party conducts the intervention. Even if the leader doesn't intervene directly in the process, or during mediation, his contribution is still important. Here are some suggestions on what role to assume in this context.

Advice for the leader

- *Let go of the "if."* "If I had done this, I could have prevented …". We're no longer at the prevention stage. There is no need in you moping. You need to mourn the past and focus on the present. You'll always have time in the future to take stock of your mistakes and learn from them. But, for the moment, the war has not been won. We still need you to direct the operations and ensure that new behaviors are enforced and maintained. Now you need to fulfill your role as guardian of these new rules of conduct.

- *Transform guilt into action.* There's no point in feeling guilty or spreading the guilt around you. Doing so won't remedy the problem; in fact, it will only slow the resolution process. For example, you can say the following to your team members, "Yes, it's a shame that we've reached this point and I, too, am disappointed in the scale this conflict has reached. We need to work together toward a common goal: improving our relationships and work climate."

- *Make sure to follow up.* This is of the utmost importance. After the storm, you'll find that people involved in conflict will have only one desire: to forget the moments of turmoil. It can even happen that they won't want to talk about it, as doing so only recalls their suffering. Nevertheless, you need to strive to preserve the quality of the working environment and not consider the reactions mentioned above as proof that the issue has been settled once and for all.

- *Dare to intervene between people who partake in inappropriate behavior.* Yes, I said *intervene,* which means taking disciplinary action, in whatever way that adapts to your context. Follow up regularly; if not, you risk the unraveling of everything you've worked so hard to achieve. If this happens again, your employees will not forgive you and you'll certainly lose your credibility as a leader. You can't afford to make the same mistake twice.

Advice for the team

Without the goodwill of the team members, reconciliation is impossible. Since some of them have already left, those who stay can all the more remedy their working situation. It's up to them to change the climate during their daily interactions.

- *Accept that there won't be perfection.* Relationships and a work environment completely free of conflict do not exist. If you think that your work environment won't meet your needs, it may be time to reflect on your career direction.

- *Invest in your relationships.* Ignoring, fleeing from or avoiding the sources of misunderstanding, and, therefore, the people, is one way to withdraw. If you want to restore confidence, it's certainly not the best strategy to adopt. In his analogy of the emotional bank account, Stephen Covey suggests that we adopt the following attitude when cultivating relationships, at least if want to establish trust: *Seek to understand others before seeking to be understood.* Try, you'll see the difference.

- *Focus on small successes.* Every inch of trust gained symbolizes progress. It takes many good deeds to regain someone's trust. The situation won't completely remedy itself after three attempts. You must have patience and perseverance.

- *Dare to denounce misplaced behavior.* Yes, I said *denounce,* as in *make known.* You need to change your concept of denouncing, making sure your intentions are benevolent. If you denounce something, it's because you want to maintain a healthy work environment and harmonious relationships – you're making a gesture of affirmation. It goes without saying that your tone must be just and reflect your intentions.

An example of resolution: the conflict between professors

It's no small feat to reconcile people involved in a conflict of such large scale over such a long period of time (four years). We were able to improve the climate and relationships because several people had left the department, changing the dynamic. Others had withdrawn and others had taken a one-year sabbatical. Those departures facilitated things, because the people in question had actively participated in the conflict.

However, we were worried about the departures of those who had joined more recently and were less entangled in the conflict. We also had to take into account those who were on sick leave and their planned return to work. Their reinstatement had to be planned carefully; it had to be timed at an opportune moment so that we could manage the precarious equilibrium that is conflict. Because these people had not been involved in the resolution process, we had to ensure that their return would not once again damage the climate of the department.

Before introducing the resolution process, let's review the indicators that affected the way we consider conflict.

1. *The Exclusion Stage*

- The arrival of new team members disrupted the equilibrium that had lasted for several years.

- The delays imposed on Julie concerning her tools for work and her difficulty to integrate with the team seemed to reveal malicious intentions in some colleagues and supervisors.

- The manager was slow to react to Julie's difficulties.

2. *The Confrontation Stage*

- The integration of new employees whose expertise differed from those of their colleagues could have created insecurity in those longtime members.

- The need to redefine some rules of operation was not recognized by some. The unjust way of assigning tasks and granting privileges led to relational difficulties.

3. *The Faction-Forming Stage*

- Clans are already formed according to the affinities of each. Those who are different are excluded.

- Oppositions and differences had arisen for a long time, but were never accommodated. This was an incentive to seek more allies within the group. Even the new members could not stay out of the clans' grasp.

- The supervisor acted inappropriately when he rested on his colleagues' support just to make changes. He reinforced the opposing clan's offensive, as members already thought he was trying to impose his changes and dominate over them: They accused him of abusing his power.

4. *The Escalation and Explosion Stage*

- The triggering event was the teacher evaluation, which provoked the deterioration of work relations and reinforced unacceptable conduct.

- Hostile and inappropriate behavior was adopted: hostility, verbal threats, intimidation and defamation.

- Clans continuously attacked each other; this struggle was characterized by an interchangeability of roles, each clan in turn assuming the role of the oppressor and the oppressed.

5. *The Estrangement Stage*

- The professors' departures took place at all times: sick leave or work leave such as resignations, retirement, or requests for annual leave.

In fact, the approach taken was similar to the one I mentioned in the case of the dissolution of clans in Stage 3. Since the conflict was widespread and varied, a systematic approach was needed, as it would allow us to specify at which level we needed to intervene in order to reach a resolution. We couldn't have solved the conflict, for example, by mediating between rivals. Because the entire team had been contaminated by the conflict, we would first need to intervene between them and then continue to intervene in other areas. The process demanded much time and many resources, and created significant direct and indirect costs. Here, in order, are the steps that we took:

1. Diagnosis of the organizational climate.

2. Transmission of this diagnosis and a description of the dynamics of the team to management and all members of the department.

3. Validation of the possible solutions identified by senior management with those involved in the conflict.

4. The arrival of an external supervisor responsible for managing the department's operations.

5. Guidance of the leadership and members of the department in managing meetings, making decisions, and overall guiding the work climate.

6. The creation of a committee on the work climate, which brought together members of both clans.

7. Creation of a code of conduct created by the "climate committee" and implementation of this code by all members of the department.

8. Mediation between certain people.

9. Dissolution of clans, thanks to the efforts of the "climate committee" and diverse projects requiring the collaboration of colleagues belonging to both clans.

10. Reintegration of those who were on sick leave or sabbatical.

11. Disciplinary hearings, if necessary.

12. Election of an internal leader after the dissolution of clans (which was largely completed).

13. Following up after the intervention.

It was possible to reconcile some people. For them, the suffering became so unbearable that they needed to adhere to a goal of rebuilding the work environment in order to find hope or motivation. Thanks to them, the operation was a success. I won't hide it from you, not all of these employees became good friends. Some chose to compromise, thus defining the limits of their professional relationships: They tolerated one another as colleagues and respected one another in the workplace. Some wounds affect people so deeply that reconciliation is impossible. This is exactly the type of psychological breakdown I mentioned earlier.

Fortunately, the teaching profession does not require continuous interactions with colleagues. But, in another field of work, the degree of reconciliation that was achieved among the professors would not have sufficed. Several of them retained this lesson, "Never again will we allow our relationship to deteriorate." Even the most combative members forfeited their arms in the last stretch, which resulted in unexpected success.

Resolution tools adapted to this stage

You're wondering what you can do to avoid this type of estrangement? Here are some ideas.

- *Intervening in the team.* Rebuild the team, and revive confidence by focusing on creating a new dynamic thanks to the arrival of some and the departure of others.

- *Intervening in the organization.* An unhealthy climate could have reached other groups in the organization. Supporting the leaders presents a great opportunity to prevent the situation from happening again elsewhere.

- *Time.* The old saying goes, "Time heals all wounds." However, unacceptable behaviors must have ceased before time can play a role in reconciliation.

Summary

Stage 5: Estrangement

Dismemberment of a team, literally or figuratively.

	Symptoms/Indicators Present	Tools and Techniques to Prevent Estrangement	Indicators of Improvement
Type of Energy	•Absent	---	•Reconstructive energy
Climate	•Apathetic, cold	•Consult experts in conflict resolution and mediation •Consult with trade unions and obtain their cooperation •Don't intervene single handedly	•A decrease in departures or demands for vacation time
Communication	•Lack of communication between those who have ended their relationships	•Explain each step of the resolution process and specify each person's role	•Reestablishing communication among those who severed their ties
Interpersonal relations	•Estranged relationships or dismissals, resulting in lost time and financial resources	•Diagnose the situation by meeting with all people involved	•The parties involved attempt to turn the page by not dwelling on past issues
Work Teams	•Lack of teamwork because numerous personnel have left, abuse of vacation time, sabotage between opposing individuals	•Encourage the participation of the people involved in the resolution	•Most of the people are invested in resolving the conflict •Parties involved commit to respecting the plan of action and code of conduct, elaborated by the start of reconciliation and resolution
Attitudes	•"I couldn't care less."	•Develop strategies designed to restore the work climate and everyone's trust	•Willingness of the parties to put an end to the "war zone" and a commitment: a more constructive approach
Needs	•Self-protection, recovering self-esteem	•Thank certain players	•Several members of the team recognize the need for reconciliation

Estrangement ◄───► Reconciliation

Frequent Reactions

From the Team	From the Leader
Quitting, leaving the team	Reacting at the last minute
Adopting avoidant behavior: ignoring or refusing to talk to someone; refusing to collaborate or work with that person	Professional exhaustion
	Quitting, fleeing during the shipwreck

CHAPTER 6: VARIABLES ASSOCIATED WITH CONFLICT

In this final chapter, we will cover some key principles that are associated with conflict:

- Time

- Needs

- Power and leadership

- Costs

- Prevention

- Management styles

We'll also present a basic overview of mediation.

Time

First key principle: Time is conflict resolution's worst enemy.

As more time passes, the conflict begins to involve more people. By examining Stage 3, which is the formation of factions, we were able to note that an unresolved interpersonal conflict can worsen and take hold of more people. The tipping point between interpersonal conflict and team conflict is at Stage 3.

A word of advice: If you want to limit the negative impact of interpersonal conflict, the best thing to do is to act quickly.

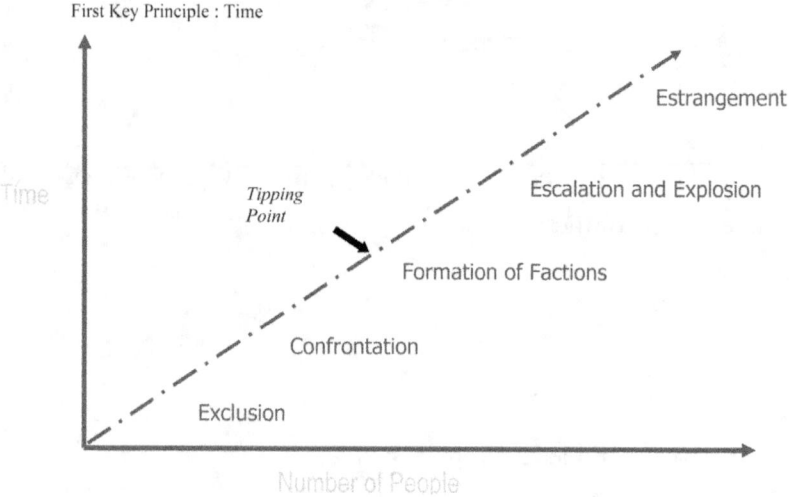

Needs

The second key principle is simple: The evolution of conflict involves an accumulation of unmet needs.

This accumulation, in turn, causes even more frustration. As time passes, the sources of conflict increase, and it becomes more complex. For this reason, trying to resolve a conflict after Stage 3 is very difficult. Several layers of unmet needs are intertwined.

The following diagram shows the relationship between underlying needs and the evolution of conflict.

Second Key Principle : Needs

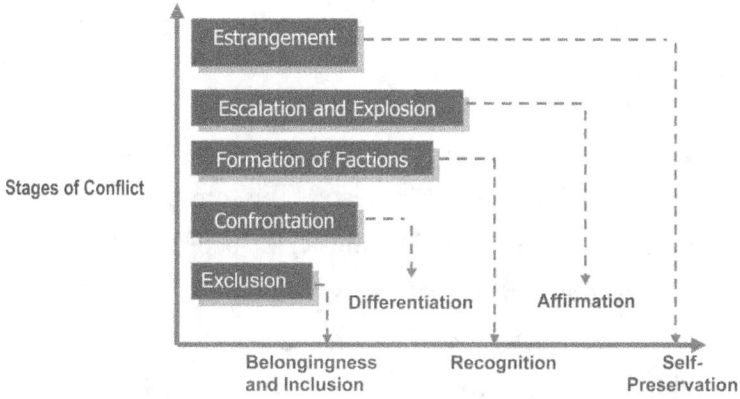

Unmet Needs

So, at **Stage 1**, the first level of relational unease – which we called exclusion – is generated from the need for belonging and inclusion. This stage doesn't necessarily lead to the outbreak of conflict.

At **Stage 2**, confrontation reflects the diverse needs of the people involved, which applies to the way they do things and integrate with a team. This need can manifest itself in various forms: It can be ways an individual exercises his role or takes his place, exposes his ideas and opinions, applies certain rules or methods of working, etc. Confronting those needs is an important stage in the evolution and maturation of a work team. The better members are at managing their differences, the more they can evolve toward a higher level of maturity, and, as a result, benefit from those differences.

If the previous stage fails, the people involved in a conflict will seek to have the *legitimacy of their needs recognized.* Those who are trying to justify their increasingly pressing needs have a contaminating effect on their peers. The more needs at stake, the greater the motivation to seek the support of their colleagues. So, when people adopt this sort of behavior, clans form and define themselves as opposing entities. The formation of factions, in **Stage 3**, is motivated by one objective: Each group wants to exercise its power over the others in order to have its own needs *recognized.*

By coming together, individuals have greater influence. When clans battle, their striking power is greater. The summation of conflict leads to escalation. The need that motivates people in **Stage 4** of conflict is *affirmation.* The protagonists, stubbornly seeking to assert their existence and respective positions, defend themselves; they'll stop at nothing to win. Furthermore, at this stage, their needs reflect little consideration for the other parties. "You must comply with our expectations" succinctly demonstrates the prevailing spirit. And these expectations reflect the values that come up. Escalation leads to tactics that become increasingly violent and hurtful. The antagonists claim that they're fighting because the other clan attacked them, intimidated them, or caused them unnecessary grief. Their needs have been transformed into false beliefs that unite the complicit parties. By accusing the other of malicious intentions, each clan justifies its own reactions.

As more altercations transpire, there is a more imminent risk of estrangement. The numerous wounds lead to greater emotional involvement and susceptibility. In **Stage 5**, estrangement seems to be the only option for the clans to protect themselves from future attacks and injuries. Since most people no longer recognize themselves in their new actions and roles, they have only one need at this point: *preserving their self-image and self-esteem.* And, they do so by distancing themselves from those who cause them suffering.

Power and leadership

The third key principle: As conflict evolves, the more power the people involved seek to gain, and the more the leadership's power is lost.

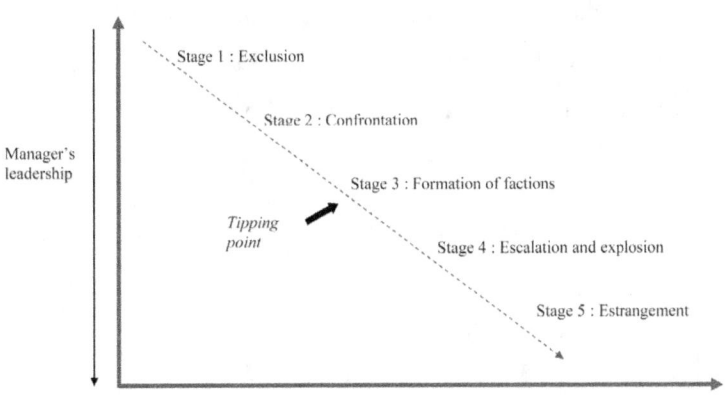

Third Key Principle: Power and Leadership

In our previous explanation of Stage 3, we saw that opponents aim to win using their power. Power struggles impede just leadership within a team. Clans blame the managers for not resolving the conflict and ending a painful situation. Having lost sight of their personal responsibility in managing their relationships, the teams charge the manager with this task. The result: The manager is "put on trial" – he's incapable of managing his team or the work climate. His credibility and leadership are weakened. The more the manager's leadership is challenged, the easier it is for him to feel unable to manage the situation. Thus, a vicious circle is formed.

Costs

The fourth key principle: The longer the conflict endures, the more significant the costs and efforts will be, and it will take an intervention, at numerous levels, to resolve it.

This principle supports everything we have discussed until now, especially the examples of conflict resolution at Stages 3, 4 and 5. The regulation of a widespread conflict requires multiple interventions, done at different levels, as shown in the following graphic.

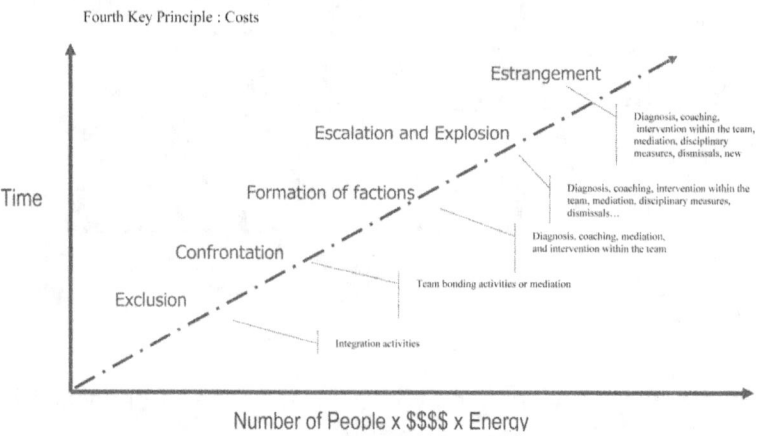

Prevention

The fifth key principle: The quicker the manager intervenes, the better his chances of preventing and defusing the team's conflicts.

The following diagram shows the periods where the manager can intervene efficiently, meaning, he can limit the interpersonal conflicts before they begin to affect the work and relational climates. Therefore, during Stages 1, 2, and 3 of conflict (exclusion, confrontation, beginning of the formation of factions), preventative steps can still be taken. By exercising proactive leadership at these stages, the manager can stop or decelerate the evolution of conflict within his team. If the conflict tips toward Stage 4, prevention is no longer possible. Using external resources will be necessary to reverse the confrontational dynamic that has spread throughout the team.

Fifth Key Principle : Prevention

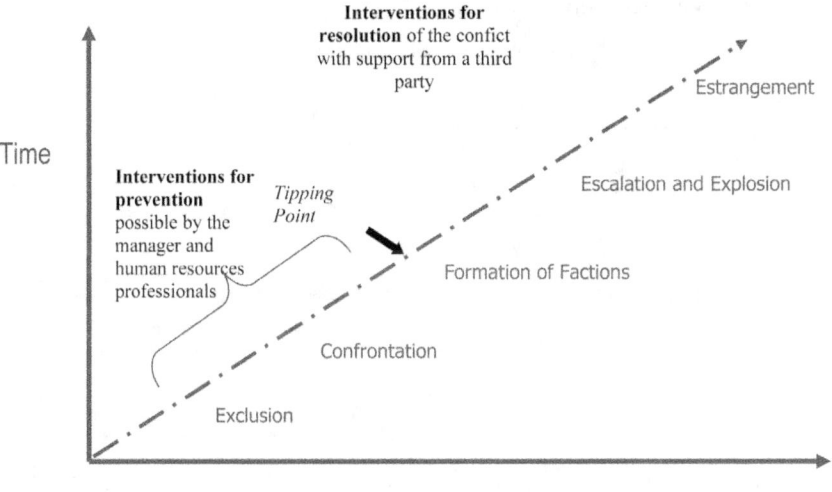

Number of people X $$$$ X energy

Management styles

The sixth key principle: By intervening quickly, the manager can reverse the conflict's process and ensure a harmonious work environment.

Adopting a reactive style of management doesn't necessarily lead to a conflict's outbreak. The context, the people involved and their experiences, as well as other variables will affect the way we can surmount relational difficulties. For example, a work environment that encourages competition can tolerate, even welcome, conflicting ideas and values.

When organizations concern themselves with their organizational climate (it happens, thankfully!) and support their managers, they act positively on the work climate. The stages of the deterioration of a climate are presented below in pyramid form in order to show you how to transform your work environment by adopting the appropriate management style.

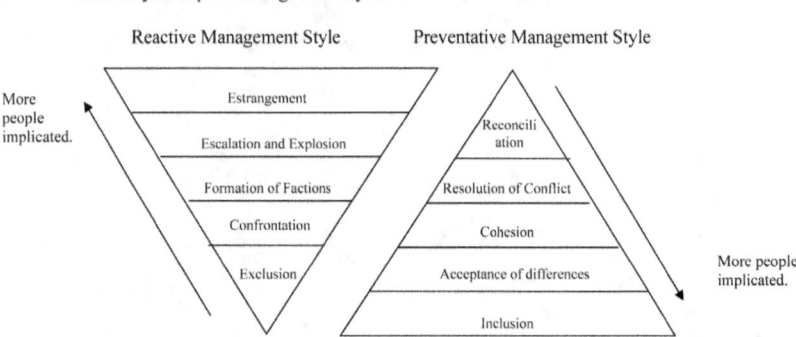

Sixth Key Princple : Management Styles

Reactive Management Style   Preventative Management Style

More people implicated.

Estrangement
Escalation and Explosion
Formation of Factions
Confrontation
Exclusion

Reconciliation
Resolution of Conflict
Cohesion
Acceptance of differences
Inclusion

More people implicated.

How can you attempt more prevention? The answer is simple: by adopting conduct that constantly concerns itself with preserving the quality of the interpersonal relationships and work climate. Some managers have great listening skills, know how to show empathy, and are comfortable at managing disputes. Without realizing it, they react naturally in such situations and are able to defuse the conflicts. For others, these skills are not as developed.

Mediation is a prevention strategy within every manager's reach. When relational difficulties arise between two people, it's easier to act. By intervening as a mediator, we can defuse the localized conflict before it spreads to the team.

Mediation: an overview

There are excellent resources dedicated solely to mediation. I thought it would be wise to briefly discuss the technique by emphasizing the conditions and needs that are important to retain throughout the process, as well as the stages of the process of mediation.

This section offers the answers to the six most frequently asked questions about mediation.

1. *Who* does mediation address?

2. *When* is it best to mediate a conflict?

3. *Why* mediation?

4. *What topics should be discussed,* and what are the conditions for success?

5. *Where* should we undertake mediation?

6. *How* does the mediation process unfold?

Who does mediation address?

Mediation is for people who have a dispute, but only if it is great enough to prevent them from working together. For mediation to succeed, it's important that the parties be willing to dedicate themselves to the process. The person acting as mediator must facilitate the situation by acting in the most impartial and objective way.

Rules and Conditions for the Mediator
Act with impartiality.
Remain objective regarding the subject of the dispute. Avoid choosing sides.
Clearly explain the mediation process to the parties involved.
Specify the role and limits of the intervention.
Discuss alternative solutions to mediation, and the consequences of its failure.
Make time.
Master the skills of facilitation: listening, empathizing, clearly communicating, synthesizing, etc.
Guarantee the confidentiality of the discussion.
Remain credible.

Rules and Conditions for the Protagonists
Commit to the mediation process.
Make yourself available.
Invest yourself personally and emotionally.
Respect the conditions for success: openness, respect, adherence to confidentiality agreement.
Be willing to try a mode of conflict resolution different from that which would be spontaneously adopted.
Trust the mediator, who must be credible.

When is it best to mediate a conflict?

The sooner the better. When we act quickly to resolve a dispute or unease between people, the intervention can be quick. We can recall the words of a team leader, previously cited, who intervened within his team at the first signs of unease. He invited them to speak openly and clearly state their needs and expectations. In this way, he prevented a serious conflict. A more structured intervention may be necessary when persistent relational difficulties can't be solved by simply inviting people to speak. In this case, greater effort is needed to bring out the real needs of the people involved in the dispute, because even they may not see them clearly.

Why mediation?

Mediation aims to actively involve the parties in finding a solution to their dispute. Why hold mediation rather than allowing the manager to choose the solution? Because the solutions proposed by each party emerge during an intervention. The solutions will evolve until an agreement is made that reflects the needs of the opposing groups. Furthermore, mediation fosters a greater respect for the agreement since the parties did not have to submit to a decision made by a third party, such as the manager. Another advantage: By participating in mediation, each person can discover the perception that the other party holds, and the effect of his behavior on the other. It's a perfect opportunity to obtain feedback and grow on a personal level. If the mediation succeeds, the people involved will have learned to manage their disputes and emotions constructively, and they'll be better prepared to defuse other conflicts.

Advantages of Mediation
Greater commitment to implementing solutions
Solutions take into account both parties' objective and subjective realities.
New way to solve conflict
Opportunity for feedback
Opportunity to heal wounds, restore relationships based on trust

Misconceptions About Mediation That Protagonists Need to Dispel
Mediation…
…gives the opposing parties a chance to negotiate.
…benefits the party that holds the most power or has the most seniority.
…is a disguised way to compel parties to compromise.
…will force the parties to reveal weaknesses or emotions.

What topics should be discussed, and what are the conditions for success?

All contentious issues can be addressed during mediation. It should be noted that the real issues are not always clear at the beginning and may change in the process. It is therefore important to frequently consult the parties to determine the relevance of topics for discussion and to devote the appropriate amount of time. It may also appear that seemingly irrelevant information, or information that doesn't seem to be factual, is being mediated, but subjective information is just as important as any other.

Indeed, the process is more likely to succeed if participants consider all the impressions, emotions, reactions toward change, values, and needs rather than just the desired solution. Very often, mediation fails because the emphasis on finding a solution is premature and the parties' perceptions (objective and subjective) are not taken into consideration. In other cases, mediation doesn't evolve because the mediator (manager) places too much importance on the causes of the conflict. This method incites parties to argue about the past. The mediator must quickly refocus the situation to concentrate on the present moment and desired situation.

Possible Subjects for Mediation	
Objective Realities	**Subjective Realities**
Perception of goals	Perceptions of each party
Facts, events, impact	Needs
Expectations	Values
Interests	Emotional reactions
Desired situation	Discussion of the two parties' perceived strengths and weaknesses
Foreseeable solutions	
Conditions for success	
Constraints	

Tips to Improve the Chance of Success
Create an open and trusting climate.
Specify the objectives, rules of conduct, and each person's role.
Listen empathetically when the parties speak emotionally.
Respect each person's rhythm, act with flexibility.
Maintain respectful and open attitudes throughout the entire process.
Choose a suitable environment.
Know how to refocus an issue.
Direct the conversation toward the present and the desired situation.
Guide the parties toward a constructive approach to solving their dispute.
Manage the exchange and reflect the underlying emotions.
Hold each party accountable in his or her part of the issue.
Encourage the parties' commitment to the agreement.
Avoid generating negative emotions (hurt, blame, doubt, etc.).

Factors That Contribute to Failure
Trying to go too fast
Not listening
Assigning a rigid time frame; not being flexible
Postponing the meetings because of a lack of preparation or not adhering to the time
Placing too much emphasis of the causes of conflict, the past
Letting too much time elapse between meetings (for example, more than four weeks)
Imposing solutions as a mediator
Acting without the criteria needed as a mediator: trust, impartiality, credibility

Where should we undertake mediation?

The location can, without a doubt, influence the evolution of the mediation. For example, if the individuals meet in your office and are constantly interrupted, it will minimize your ability to listen. On that same note, if the parties feel that everyone in the office knows of their situation, they may feel awkward about meeting in their manager's office. Choose a neutral environment where the discussion won't be disturbed, and one that favors openness. I like to conduct mediations in a human resources office, conference room, or even in a room at a hotel. Taking a step back from the work environment can help foster a certain emotional distance, which is a good thing in this case.

How does the mediation process unfold?

Here are the steps of the mediation process. The following table will offer a more detailed description of each step.

1. Initial contact

2. Data collection

3. Refocusing and summary report

4. Preparation of the first meeting (three parties)

5. Subsequent meetings (as many as necessary)

6. Summary of agreements

7. Post-mediation follow-up

Summary

Steps in the Process	Goals Pursued	Questions Addressed	Results Attempted
1. Initial Contact	•Check to ensure that parties involved are interested in commit to the mediation process •Explain the process and its possible advantages to both parties •Obtain the consent of both parties	•Interest •Trust •Willingness to commit	•Clear agreement between both parties in their approach to mediation and an indication of maturity
2. Data Collection	•Hear both parties individually •Learn their versions of the facts, emotions, and consequences of a lack or failure of mediation •Determine the practicality of mediation	•Facts •Perceptions •Emotions •Consequences, impacts •Interests •Needs and expectations •Values •Personal limits •Desired situation •Envisioned solutions •Conditions of success and its constraints •Clarification of roles	•Portrayal of a conflicting dynamic, including the conditions of success and factors risked
3. Refocusing and Summary Report	•Restate the problem by distinguishing between facts and perceptions •Summarize, in writing, the elements of the problematic conflict	•Facts •Perceptions: convergent and divergent points •List of each party's expectations •Way that the mediator perceives the actual conflict •Solutions: envisioned or points to improve on	•Succinct report written in a constructive manner and presenting the principle elements of the conflicting dynamic the way it has been refocused
4. Preparation of the First Meeting (Three Parties)	•Present the report and start a dialogue on the perceptions • Note each party's reaction on the issues presented •Agree on the way the meetings will proceed	•Reports of the stages •Rules of the "game" and strategies •Changes that each person is willing to make •Addressing resistance •Dates and times	•Open-mindedness: each party is prepared to consider the others' point of view •Opportunity to address other issues that may affect the mediation
5. Subsequent Meetings (as Many as Necessary)	•Create a trusting environment •Restore communication between parties •Progressively mention the points that need improvement •Encourage the participation of the parties in creating solutions that take into account both parties' realities	•Determination of ways to build confidence •Feedback exercises focusing on each party's perceived strengths •Exploration of individual differences and similarities •Discussion on points to improve •Agreements on the envisioned solutions	•Individual and group engagements relative to the agreements negotiated in the course of mediation
6. Summary of the Agreements	•Write an account of the individual and common agreements and confirm the validity of these accounts by consulting with the parties	•Agreements •Conditions conducive to the respect of agreements	•Remittance of reports and planning of follow-ups
7. Post-Mediation Follow-Up	•Follow up on the evolution of the parties' relationships and their compliance with the agreements made •Emphasize the lessons learned	•Assessment of achievements and successes. Assessment of lessons learned. Discovery of new expectations	•End of the mediation process

CONCLUSION

In order to provide managers and team members an approach that promotes conflict- prevention and healthy management of the work environment, I wanted to present the milestones in the evolution of the approach. I also indicated at what stage managers can act preventively without taking on too much risk. Each conflict is unique and so is its resolution. Don't take what has been suggested as a blanket solution or one created in advance; I prefer to provide examples of conflicts dissected at various phases of their progress. Moreover, the information on these cases has been filtered, so to speak, so that each can illustrate one of the stages of conflict. Realistically, conflicts are not as clear-cut as those presented in this book.

Because any conflict involves perceptions, people, and its own context, I also wanted to illustrate the shared responsibility between the manager and his or her team regarding the work environment. After all, it is a result of the day-to-day interactions of those who work together. Through their words and actions, they exercise a lot of power: that of influencing their work environment.

Yes, conflicts can be positive, and we can gain some benefit from them. If, with the support of their manager, the team members are able to surmount their relational difficulties and disputes, they'll derive pleasure from working together.

Finally, I hope to have accomplished my goal and that this book has shown you the positive side of conflict. On my part, my sailing experience allowed me to make some great discoveries. The first is that not only can conflict be dissected into stages, but its local manifestation (between two people) can differ from its global one (within the whole group). The second is that neutrality is impossible in a team conflict. Sooner or later, the clans will put pressure on the team members who wish to stay out of it.

What happened to the Lilly?

Are you wondering what happened to the *Lilly's* crew after the estrangement stage? Would you like to know how the rest of the crew got along during the last seven days of the voyage?

After the departure of the three young crew members, we lived, for a short two days, a sort of honeymoon period. Then, reality caught up. On my part, I mentioned my doubts in the captain's ability to manage the climate on board. In fact, he continued to disappoint us with his lack of organization and assiduity. He frequently failed to meet his promises.

After a long internal debate, caught between feelings of guilt at the idea of abandoning my fellow crew members during the hardest course (two days of 12-hour navigations each) and my own needs, I decided to choose myself. I abandoned the *Lilly* on Day 12 and finally got to relax on a seven-day holiday on the isle of Syros. I also got to reflect on what had been a rather tumultuous situation. I crept off like a thief, at dusk, after saying my goodbyes to Guy and Sylvie, and without saying anything to the captain, who was out with the islanders.

After the vacation ended, my friends Guy and Sylvie shared with me the final disappointments they experienced during the end of the voyage. It seemed that, despite a strict navigation course, the captain, as usual, didn't respect his agreements regarding the morning departures – his nights out at the bars made it hard for him to wake up in time.

You can be sure that my sailing experience did not end the day I disembarked from the *Lilly*. It stayed with me for quite some time and motivated me to write this book. If it's true that we can learn from most of our experiences, then the *Lilly's* story is no exception. By breaking up the crew, we got rid of the symptoms, but not the problem. Suppressing the symptoms of a conflict doesn't necessarily result in a resolution of the conflicting dynamic. As I mentioned before, you need to react in the right degree.

As for me, each attempt at a resolution that I make as a "conflict management specialist," each group situation that I enter as a team member, allows me the chance to improve myself. It is up to each of us to transform the unfortunate reality that is conflict into an opportunity of development and improvement.

SUGGESTED READING

BLANCHARD, Kenneth and Sheldon BOWLES. *High Five! The Magic of Working Together*, New York, Harper Collins, 2001, 203 p.

BRIGGS MYERS, Isabel and Peter B. MYERS. *Gifts Differing: Understanding Personality Type*, Palo Alto, California, Davies-Black Publishing, 1980, 228 p.

CORMIER, Solange. *Dénouer les conflits relationnels en milieu de travail* (From French: *Defusing Relational Conflicts in the Workplace)*, Sainte-Foy, Presses, l'Université du Québec, 2004, 188 p.

COVEY, Stephen. *Les sept habitudes de ceux qui réalisent tout ce qu'ils entreprennent* (From French: *The Seven Habits of Highly Successful People)*, Paris, Éditions générales FIRST, 1996, 320 p.

DELUNAS, Eve. *Survival Games Personalities Play*, Carmel, California, Sunflower Ink, 1992, 283 p.

LABELLE, Ghislaine. *Une équipe du tonnerre* (From French: *A Winning Team)*, Montréal, Les Éditions Transcontinental et Les Éditions de la Fondation de l'Entrepreneurship, 2001, 175 p.

LANDAU, Sy, Barbara LANDAU and Daryl LANDAU. *From Conflict to Creativity*, San Francisco, California, Jossey-Bass, 2001, 187 p.

MARQUIER, Annie. *Le pouvoir de choisir* (From French: *The Power of Choice),* Knowlton, Québec, Les Éditions Universelles du Verseau, 1991, 281 p.

MYERS, E. Gail and Michele Tolela MYERS. *Les bases de la communication interpersonnelle: une approche théorique et pratique* (From French: *The Basics of Interpersonal Communication: Theory and Practical Approach),* Montréal, McGRAWHILL, Éditeurs, 1984, 461 p.

PERKINS, N. T. Dennis. *Leadership sous 0°* (From French: *Leadership Below Zero Degrees).* Gatineau, Éditions du Trésor caché, 2003, 236 p.

POITRAS, Jean and André LADOUCEUR. *Systèmes de gestion de conflits* (From French: *Systems of Conflict Management),* Cowansville, Québec, Éditions Yvon Blais, 2004, 185 p.

SAINT-ARNAUD, Yves. *Les petits groupes: participation et communication* (From French: *Small Groups: Participation and Communication),* Montréal, Les Presses de l'Université de Montréal, Les Éditions du CIM, 1978, 176 p.

STONE, Douglas, et al, *Difficult Conversations: How to Discuss What Matters Most,* New York, Penguin Books, 2000, 250 p.

THOMAS, Kenneth W. and Ralph H. KILMANN. *Méthode Thomas-Kilmann d'évaluation du comportement en situation de conflit* (From French: *Thomas-Kilmann Conflict Mode Instrument),* Mountain View, California, CPP Inc., 17 p., also distributed in Canada by Psychometrics Canada.

WEISINGER, Hendrie. *L'intelligence émotionnelle au travail: gérer ses émotions et améliorer ses relations avec les autres* (From French: *Emotional Intelligence at Work: Managing Emotions and Improving Relationships With Others)*, Montréal, Les Éditions Transcontinental, 1998, 235 p.

Footnotes

1 The Myers-Briggs Type Indicator (MBTI) is based on Jung's theory of psychological type and reports your preferences on four scales. This tool is often used to explore different strengths in a team context.

2 At this stage, team-bonding exercises serve as excellent means to allow the members of your teams to evolve and discover their differences. For more information, see Ghislaine Labelle, A Winning Team (translated from French: Une équipe du tonnerre).

3 THOMAS, Kenneth W. and Ralph H. KILMANN, *The Thomas-Kilmann Conflict Mode Instrument*, Mountain View, California, CPP Inc., 1974.

4 I prefer to start with individual meetings. But, we can organize a meeting of all three members if the situation is not characterized by too many issues and the element of trust is not completely damaged.

Ghislaine is available to speak to your
business or organization.

To learn more visit: www.calmingthewatersatwork.com.

She lives in Montréal, Québec
with her beautiful Golden Retriever Pablo
and enjoys sailing, hiking and skiing.

She can also be reached at (514) 990-2264.

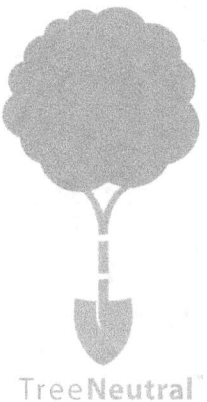

TreeNeutral